Reflective Goa

Cheryl J. Travers

Reflective Goal Setting

An Applied Approach to Personal and Leadership Development

Cheryl J. Travers
School of Business and Economics
Loughborough University
Loughborough, UK

ISBN 978-3-030-99230-9   ISBN 978-3-030-99228-6 (eBook)
https://doi.org/10.1007/978-3-030-99228-6

© The Editor(s) (if applicable) and The Author(s), under exclusive licence to Springer Nature Switzerland AG 2022
This work is subject to copyright. All rights are solely and exclusively licensed by the Publisher, whether the whole or part of the material is concerned, specifically the rights of translation, reprinting, reuse of illustrations, recitation, broadcasting, reproduction on microfilms or in any other physical way, and transmission or information storage and retrieval, electronic adaptation, computer software, or by similar or dissimilar methodology now known or hereafter developed.
The use of general descriptive names, registered names, trademarks, service marks, etc. in this publication does not imply, even in the absence of a specific statement, that such names are exempt from the relevant protective laws and regulations and therefore free for general use.
The publisher, the authors and the editors are safe to assume that the advice and information in this book are believed to be true and accurate at the date of publication. Neither the publisher nor the authors or the editors give a warranty, expressed or implied, with respect to the material contained herein or for any errors or omissions that may have been made. The publisher remains neutral with regard to jurisdictional claims in published maps and institutional affiliations.

Cover pattern © John Rawsterne/ patternhead.com

This Palgrave Pivot imprint is published by the registered company Springer Nature Switzerland AG.
The registered company address is: Gewerbestrasse 11, 6330 Cham, Switzerland

To my daughters, Elizabeth and Eleanor—two wonderful, goal-driven, soft, and interpersonally skilled young women.

Preface

'Reflective Goal Setting'—the subject of this book—is the result of almost 30 years of my engagement with teaching and research in personal and leader development. This is the first time that the model has been shared in such detail outside of the lecture theatre or training room and is imparted in the sincere hope that many more people can benefit from this powerful, award-winning, and well used 'toolkit' for personal and leader transformation. Up until now, it has been used predominantly as a transfer of learning framework in educational contexts, been the focus of academic outputs, been talked about in keynote addresses, and been shared via TEDx. It has also been readily discussed with anyone I have encountered who was eager to know how to create relevant, challenging, and often life-changing goals.

There is some trepidation, as I have usually had a major hand in how the model is delivered—my passion and the enthusiasm of a team of coaches in the School of Business and Economics at Loughborough University, UK, has driven it forward and seen amazing results. But in more recent times, others have also employed it in their teaching, consulting, coaching, and research. So, I feel it is time to share it via this medium. The book is a juxtaposition of academic rationale and practical know-how and how-to. So, I am confident that this book will empower people to utilize it effectively and with the same level of energy and enthusiasm as myself and others have embraced it.

My belief is that if we give people a clear framework that shows them how to choose, set and write about personal and leader development goals successfully, they can enjoy greater independence when working on aspects of themselves in both work and non-work contexts. Couple that with illustrations and evidence of how something works in practice, and they will be motivated to do so. Add in strong psychological theory, and we have the bonus of trust that something is not just a fad and is worth working on. Psychology is there to be shared with those who are the subject of it, people. As an academic Occupational Psychologist, I am passionate about 'giving Psychology away'—be that with undergraduates, postgraduates, or organisational leaders and managers returning to learning. Shared authentically, empathically, and ethically, psychological theory has a lot to offer practically and can be released into the capable hands of those who may benefit most and not just shared with other academics in prestigious journals and texts.

The book is the result of many years of teaching, research, and use of strong psychological theory. It is littered with concepts and references to other scholars' contributions in the field but is not an in-depth, critical literature review of those contributions. Rather, it presents a selection of relevant theories and models which have influenced the development of the model, and/or been shared in teaching sessions with reflective goal setters. It is designed to enable the reader to firstly gain a grasp of the key psychological concepts and models which have influenced its design, and secondly, to apply that knowledge immediately to a variety of contexts and situations. It offers a balance between theory and application and encourages evidenced-based practice from the reader.

So, Reflective Goal Setting is a theory-driven, practical five-stage approach for enhancing self-awareness and the ideation, development, and implementation of personal development goals underpinned by ongoing written reflection on goal activity. Reflective Goal Setting is about behaviour, attitude, and psychological change. If you have ever wanted to: Say no when others put pressure on you to do something you didn't want to do? Feel less stressed? Become more confident? Stop comparing yourself to others? Think more positive thoughts? Create a better impression? Get healthier? Influence others to do what you want? Be a genuinely better leader? Be happier in your own skin? Secure that job? Achieve that higher grade? Improve your relationships, then Reflective Goal Setting could help you turn those desires into achievable goals

Based in Business Schools throughout my career, I have been fortunate to have worked with a wide variety of talented students and business managers and leaders across a wide range of industry sectors. Business schools are expected to prepare their learners for effectiveness in industry and successful future leadership. A significant challenge facing business education providers is their ability to design and deliver programmes that effectively address current and future skill sets of frontline managers and produce graduates that can operate in changing environments. A growing emphasis on learner-centred education and work-based learning challenges business schools to develop stretching, engaging, and innovative educational experiences that support the transfer of learning from the classroom back into the workplace to enhance personal and organisational performance. Innovative pedagogical and andragogical strategies are needed to effectively leverage the specialised knowledge, competences, and skill sets which leaders and managers bring as programme participants. It is also important that business school courses teach 'leaders in the making' the personal and life skills they will need to be effective in all manner of work settings. This is not exclusive to business students, however. Students from any academic discipline will enter the world of work and be required to display quality crucial 'soft skills' to help them navigate and shine in fast-paced organisational contexts.

A key motivation in the design of Reflective Goal Setting was my desire to enable my students to achieve real impact beyond my classroom. Yet, I came to realise that effective approaches to learning transfer are relatively sparse in higher educational settings. Instead, there is a distinct lack of focus on translation of learning into real-world practice. In addition, several classic theories and frameworks for behaviour change and personal development fall short in terms of their effectiveness with certain types of crucial skills—those we call 'soft' in nature.

Early on in my career, I noted that these certain skills, though misleadingly labelled 'soft', were the hardest of all to train, develop, and sustain. It became clear to me that the knowledge and practice of key softer skills were not only frequently lacking in my students, but also in the managers and leaders I encountered who were already in key organizational roles. As effective approaches to helping them improve were inadequate, I started to seek out ways to successfully enhance these soft skills—in particular, those which involved interpersonal and interactive behaviours. After studying stress in the workplace for several years, I felt certain that developing skills for more effective interactions with others, managing ours and others' emotions, dealing with conflict, self-regulating our behaviours, developing our mindsets, etc., were key to our happiness, well-being, productivity, resilience, employability, and leadership. Once I started working more in this area, I found an appreciative and hungry audience. There were so many skills, behaviours, and attitudes that people wanted to improve on, and, with my unfolding approach, they could work on these with great results. Add into the pot my own education, past experiences, and work as an academic occupational psychologist and the result was Reflective Goal Setting.

This book will develop your ability to become a 'self-coach', showing you how to set goals on any skill, at any time, without having to rely on the opportunity to attend an expensive and/or time-consuming training course. Using this text, I believe that the reader can go through the process for themselves and then confidently use it to support others in the classroom, coaching, or training context. It does not aim to cover in-depth theories and material on the soft skills themselves (such as communication skills, conflict management, etc.), though many of these will be covered as we go through the stages of the model and in case illustrations. Psychology spends a great deal of time on developing and critiquing theories and not enough on sharing peoples' stories. Anyone who has been taught by me or spent time with me socially knows that I love using stories to make a point. There will be lots of stories of peoples' Reflective Goal Setting throughout this text. This is largely possible because a key component of Reflective Goal Setting is writing reflectively about our goals, as we work on them. The result is vast pages of goal setting diaries at my disposal (with ethical approval and goal setter permission), which outline on-going attempts at goals and outcomes.

Throughout, some similar experiential exercises and reflective activities as used by my reflective goal setters will be shared, so that you can develop a good working knowledge of the model for yourselves and to use with others. In addition, you will gain the self-awareness that underpins Reflective Goal Setting. As Benjamin Franklin famously said, *'There are three things extremely hard: steel, a diamond, and to know one's self'* (Poor Richard' s Almanac, 1750.). He could have said 'four' and added in 'soft skills.'

Having assumed I was banging the writing about goals drum alone for many years, an encounter with Professor Gary Latham at a British Psychological Society annual conference in Brighton in the UK some ten years ago led to me becoming connected with other like-minded enthusiasts. Having attended a presentation of my work, Gary invited me to contribute a chapter to his and Professor Edwin Locke's latest edited work, *New Directions in Personal Goal Setting and Development* (2013). This led to a network of fellow researchers who also know the importance of writing about our goals. That network is based on academic debate, mentoring, collaboration and friendship. Ed has been especially instrumental in keeping our writing about goals drum sounding and is a great mentor and friend.

So, let's start Reflective Goal Setting!

> "By recording your dreams and goals on paper, you set in motion the process of becoming the person you most want to be. Put your future in good hands—your own."—Mark Victor Hansen

Loughborough, UK   Cheryl J. Travers

ACKNOWLEDGEMENTS

Before starting to share Reflective Goal Setting with you, it is important to acknowledge all those reflective goal setters who have put their trust in me to support their acquisition of skills over the years. They have enthusiastically and kindly allowed their goals, reflective diaries, and reports to be accumulated by me to share for the benefit of others. Students have become reflective goal setters from all walks of life: on leadership and management programmes and undergraduate and postgraduate degrees. It has never failed to amaze me how open and honest they have been when given the chance to talk about themselves and their development. My role has been to support their journeys and I have felt privileged to be able to do so. Several of their voices will be anonymously heard throughout the pages of the book. Thanks too must go to the organisations who supported their leaders' and managers' Reflective Goal Setting journeys and put faith in my approach.

My thanks must also extend to all of those who have worked with me over the years on the courses where Reflective Goal Setting has been designed and delivered, helping me coach, and gathering data. Seeing hundreds of students on one-to-ones. Their knowledge of psychological theory and how to help people in their goal development has really required a 'deep dive' into the depths of their knowledge. Special mention of one in particular, my wonderful true friend and a fabulous coach—the late George Hespe, also known to student goal setters as 'The Legend!'.

Thanks must also go to those who offered academic input, support and advice on the writing of this text. Professor Alistair Cheyne for input to Chap. 11. Dr Anthea Rose, for her work on the transfer of learning for Chap. 2, and along with Professor John Arnold and Dr Joel Warburton, support with the evaluation of the impact of the model on leaders which formed the basis for Chap. 12. Also, thanks to my brother, Martin Travers, Professor Edwin Locke, and Dr Karen Maher for feedback on the text.

About the Book

This book is divided into three parts. In Part I, I begin by outlining the inspiration for and development of Reflective Goal Setting whilst examining the kinds of skills and behaviours it targets. Next, I will discuss the limitations of approaches to the transfer of learning of these skills and show how Reflective Goal Setting supports the transfer of learning. A brief review of research on goal setting follows, and especially the growing acknowledgement of the importance of writing about our goals. The final chapter in this section will define and discuss the importance of reflection and especially its impact on the success of personal and leader development goals. In Part II and across five chapters, I will detail each of the five stages of the Reflective Goal Setting model drawing on illustrative cases and interactive activities for you to develop an understanding of how to set your own reflective goals. Part III examines a selection of applications of Reflective Goal Setting on the management of stress and coping, academic growth, and leader personal development. The final chapter will conclude with some suggestions for how the model can provide a valuable resource for researchers, educators, students, leaders, coaches, and practitioners in Organisational and Industrial Psychology, Education, and Business and Management.

Contents

Part I The Development of Reflective Goal Setting   1

1 Introduction to Reflective Goal Setting   3

2 Reflective Goal Setting and the Transfer of Learning   21

3 Reflective Goal Setting, Goal Setting Theory, and the Importance of Writing About Goals   33

4 The Nature and Importance of Reflection and Keeping a Reflective Diary   47

Part II The Reflective Goal Setting Model   63

5 Stage 1: Enhancing Self-Awareness   65

6 Stage 2: Selecting Suitable Goals   85

7 Stage 3: Visualising Successful Goal Behaviours   97

8 Stage 4: Formulating a Goal Statement   111

9 Stage 5: Putting Goals into Practice   125

Part III Practical Applications of Reflective Goal Setting   137

10 Reflective Goal Setting for Managing Stress and
    Enhancing Coping   139

11 Reflective Goal Setting and Its Impact on Academic
    Growth and Performance   153

12 Reflective Goal Setting for Leader Personal Development   165

13 Conclusions   177

Index   183

About the Author

Cheryl J. Travers is Senior Lecturer in the Work and Organisation Research Group, and Director of Alumni and Lifelong Engagement within the School of Business and Economics, Loughborough University, UK. Her academic background is in occupational and organisational psychology, and she has lectured and researched in the field of work psychology for almost 30 years. Her research interests and publications include occupational stress, management of change, and the development of her Reflective Goal Setting model for personal development and the transfer of learning. She is also keen on the use of diary methodologies in research. She has extensive experience with corporate clients, was a former Director of Executive Education at Loughborough, and has designed and delivered management, leadership and team development programmes for the public, private, and voluntary sector, in addition to delivering numerous keynote lectures and two TEDx talks. She has two grown-up daughters and three dogs and loves setting goals and reflecting in her garden.

LIST OF FIGURES

Fig. 1.1	Reflective Goal Setting	5
Fig. 5.1	Johari window. Based on Luft & Ingham (1955) and Luft (1961)	71

PART I

The Development of Reflective Goal Setting

CHAPTER 1

Introduction to Reflective Goal Setting

Why Do We Need a New Approach to Setting Personal and Leader Development Goals?

Abstract In this first chapter, I will outline the inspiration for the development of '*Reflective Goal Setting*'. Stories will be shared to illustrate the evolution of this innovative and effective goal-setting framework. As it is designed to be used by students, leaders, managers, and individuals in all manner of learning situations, examples shared will reflect that. The chapter will outline the types of skills that the model seeks to work on. A brief introduction to the model will be provided, but more details will be given in Chaps. 5, 6, 7, 8, and 9.

Keywords Personal and leader development • Soft skills • Interpersonal skills • Goal setting • Transfer of learning

Introduction

Firstly, Take a Moment to Reflect

- How do you usually go about setting goals? (If at all!)
- As an example, how do you go about making New Year's Resolutions?
- Is the approach you take different when you set goals inside and outside of work?
- What types of goals do you usually set?
- Do you write them down?
- How successful are your goal attempts typically?
- What usually gets in the way of your goal success?
- What impact does your goal setting approach have on you, and others?
- What one thing could you do to improve your approach to setting goals? (Clue: Start to use Reflective Goal Setting)

"Our goals can only be reached through a vehicle of a plan, in which we must fervently believe, and upon which we must vigorously act. There is no other route to success."—Pablo Picasso

'Reflective Goal Setting' is a five-stage model created to support personal and leader development—especially in the development of 'soft' skills (see Fig. 1.1). Chapters 5, 6, 7, 8, and 9, will outline the stages in more detail, but for now and in a nutshell:

- **Enhancing self-awareness**—where we harvest any information about ourselves, our strengths and weaknesses, using personality tests, psychometrics, feedback, appraisals, even old school reports. Exploring our consistent story, we start to log these observations and thoughts down in a Reflective Goal Setting diary.
- **Selecting suitable goals**—where we focus in on a relevant specific and challenging goal area, which tallies with our personal values, and

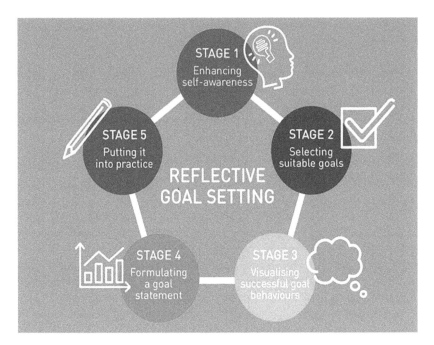

Fig. 1.1 Reflective Goal Setting

those of significant others/our organisation. We identify current scenarios and behaviours that need attention and document our findings.
- **Visualising successful goal behaviours**—where we visualise our ideal goal outcomes, how it would look and feel to be carrying out the goal successfully. Drawing on best practice and role models to help us, we identify any performance gap between how we do things now and future goal success and generate ideas for the measurement of our progress. We keep writing this down.
- **Formulating a goal statement**—where we write out our goal in detail, specific actions, techniques to apply, in what scenarios, measurement of progress, what impact we anticipate on self and others, support we might need, and from whom.
- **Putting goals into practice**—where we identify practice grounds to try out our goal wherever we can, re-adjust the goal, if necessary, continue to document our goal attempts, reviewing and evaluating

the impacts as we go along and feed this back into our self-awareness, ready to set another goal.

A key feature which leads to success with Reflective Goal Setting is this detailed writing down of goals and on-going written reflection, usually in the form of a diary kept throughout the 'lived' goal experience. We will hear more about these in Chaps. 3 and 4. But for now, I will share how the model came to be.

The Evolution of Reflective Goal Setting

Reflective Goal Setting was developed over a number of years as I worked with thousands of university undergraduate, postgraduate, and post-experience students to support their personal and skills development in my role as an academic work psychologist. Initially, the types of skills of interest to me were those of an interpersonal nature, such as communicating with others, managing conflict, working effectively in teams, enhancing leadership skills, and the whole topic of impression management in general. Klein et al. (2006, p. 81) define interpersonal skills as an umbrella term that refers to "goal directed behaviors, including communication and relationship-building competencies, employed in interpersonal interaction episodes characterized by complex perceptual and cognitive processes, dynamic verbal and nonverbal interaction exchanges, diverse roles, motivations, and expectancies." These interpersonal skills fall under the bigger umbrella of 'soft' skills. These are different to 'hard' skills which deal with the acquisition of proficiency in technical skills (such as learning how to use a particular piece of software), and instead, "Soft skills represent a dynamic combination of cognitive and meta-cognitive skills, interpersonal, intellectual and practical skills. Soft skills help people to adapt and behave positively so that they can deal effectively with the challenges of their professional and everyday life." (Haselberger et al., 2012, p. 67). Over time, the skills I was targeting expanded to cover soft skills more broadly. These are referred to in various ways, for example, 'life skills,' 'core skills,' 'employability skills.' Robles also focuses on the effects: 'Soft skills are the intangible, non-technical, personality-specific skills that determine one's strengths as a leader, facilitator, mediator, and negotiator.' (Robles, 2012, p. 457).

Working in a university provided me with first-hand experience of students' behaviours, thoughts, and feelings in a variety of settings such as lecture theatres, workshops, one-on-one personal tutor conversations, and internships visits. At the undergraduate level, I realised that despite their enthusiasm and academic abilities, students' softer skills were frequently under-developed, or even absent. For example, students often lacked the tacit knowledge for behaving professionally and confidently when working in internships. Feedback from their internship employers matched my observations—in such instances, they didn't know how to act as part of a team, how to communicate professionally, how to prioritise tasks, how to create the right impression, or present to audiences. I also realised that they lacked the '**intra**personal skills' for success, such as self-regulation, self-motivation, and having a positive mindset.

Working with managers and leaders on post-experience programmes suggested there was also a lack of these skills in those who had been working in organisations for some time. My observations suggested that a paucity of these skills was likely to cause confusion, unhappiness, conflict, stress, and poor leadership (and followership) in the workplace. Yet, insufficient focus was spent on developing these skills in the typical leadership development programme curriculum. The need for 'hard skills' development, such as how to use financial spreadsheets, always seemed to 'trump' soft, such as to actively listen.

Observations from my own research and experience were backed by others' research findings. For example, studies have shown that although graduates may display technical competencies, they may lack interpersonal skills or the ability to work effectively with others (e.g., Mourshed et al., 2012). Further, the 2012 World Economic Forum white paper reported on the substantial challenges faced by businesses attempting to recruit employees sufficiently skilled for available jobs in 67% of potential hires. Out of the 500 senior executives surveyed, 44% felt that soft skills were seriously lacking, and 56% said that they anticipated the problem getting progressively worse. The quality of graduates and their lack of soft/transferable skills, essential in today's labour market and necessary to increase individual employability, is a much-discussed debate within the literature on higher education management (Crossman & Clarke, 2010; Clarke, 2017).

Working within a university setting gave me a great opportunity to use my knowledge of work psychology to help students develop these crucial skills. However, there was a clear challenge facing those of us attempting to support such skills development. Hunt and Baruch (2003, p. 745) gathered feedback from 252 executives from 48 organizations, to evaluate management training for interpersonal skills development and concluded: "The skills most responsive to training were easily described had 'clear objectives and outcome criteria and in practice could be segmented into a step-by-step routine based on a memorable model or theory." Adding, that "The so-called soft and feely skills proved to be the most difficult to improve statistically."

When I read their findings back in 2003, I was compelled to develop an approach that could 'operationalise' and enable the development and measurement of progress in these soft and interpersonal skills—the result was Reflective Goal Setting.

There were several other pivotal experiences that inspired my thinking and the subsequent development of the model—some are from long before I embarked on my career. The underlying essence of the model and how it can be applied is probably best communicated through the following stories.

Inspiration from a School for Scoundrels

The seed for the growth of Reflective Goal Setting was sewn back when I was a youngster and clearly a budding psychologist. Tucked up on the sofa on some wet and windy Autumnal Saturday afternoon, flicking through TV channels (no remote control in those days), I chanced upon a great British black-and-white comedy from 1960 called *School for Scoundrels*. Directed by Robert Hamer, Hal E. Chester, and Cyril Frankel, the film was based on the novels of Stephen Potter and starred some great British actors of that time; my favourite being Alastair Sim as Mr S. Potter—principal of a college for 'One-Up Manship' in Yeovil, Somerset in the UK. You will have to forgive the out-dated sexism of the time in some of the description that follows.

The movie went on to tell the story of a young man, Henry Palfrey, who despite being the head of his family's firm, lacks the respect of his employees. He always seems to come unstuck in life—be it at work, love, sport—in greater part, due to his lack of interpersonal influence and skills. Reading the columns in his daily newspaper, he chances upon an advert for a special college course specialising in the essential skills to get 'one up' on others who typically stand in our way. He enrols, realises just how little he knows about influencing others successfully, learns the ropes, then sets off on a quest to put the lessons learned into operation. He swiftly and skilfully gets one over on those who have previously taken advantage of him—settling some old scores. He is on the verge of taking 'amorous' advantage of his new love interest having wooed her using a selection of his freshly acquired strategies, when he catches sight of himself mid-seduction in a nearby wall mirror and realises that he has gone too far. This 'on the spot' self-insight into these Machiavellian tendencies helps him to readdress the balance between being powerful and influential on the one hand, while maintaining respect for others and his values on the other. Using and adapting his new skills wisely to become a happier, confident man of integrity. I was gripped!

One way to examine the issues with Palfrey's development is through the lens of authenticity. Schön (1983), who I will talk about more in Chap. 4, might refer to his eureka moment mid-seduction as *'reflection-in-action'* which is where someone gains self-insight by reflecting *during* the process of carrying out a certain action, as opposed to *'reflection-on-action'*, which takes place *after* an event has occurred. A big eye-opener for me as a young person was the realisation that it was possible to learn the interpersonal skills necessary for dealing with others in all walks of life, but that these skills also had to be calibrated with our authentic self. It showed the importance of accurate and in-depth self-awareness and a knowledge of our core values before embarking on goals of this nature. There are possibly as many definitions of authenticity as there are psychologists, philosophers, and scholars. But in a nutshell, it is about living your life according to your own values and goals, rather than those of other people. Put simply, authenticity means that you are true to your own personality, values, and spirit, regardless of any pressure that you may be under to act otherwise. If you're honest with yourself and with others, and you take responsibility for your mistakes, then your values, ideals, and actions align. As a result, you come across as genuine, and you're willing to accept the consequences of being true to what you consider to be right. Some years later, I would encounter the work of leadership scholars and consultants, Rob Goffee and Gareth Jones (2000), who write about the importance of leaders being 'authentically skilled.' That, in effect, is the essence of what Reflective Goal Setting is all about.

Moment for Reflection
Have you ever tried to develop a skill only to find it feels unnatural, inauthentic, manipulative, or devious?
What was the consequence of that?
Why did you think that happened?
Were you able to re-calibrate?

Winning Friends and Influencing a Goal Setting Model

Not long after my encounter with Henry Palfrey, I came across Dale Carnegie's classic 1936 book, *How to Win Friends and Influence People*. Carnegie shared his own and others' experiences to show readers how to develop essential principles for dealing with people successfully. These focussed on key interpersonal skills, effective communication, and how to be an effective salesperson. He produced some of the earliest self-improvement manuals, and these are still popular today.

It was fascinating to read that you could work on your behaviours to become a more popular person while making others feel better about themselves too. His guidelines on such things as: how to handle people, make people like you, win people over to your way of thinking, be a leader without giving offense and resentment, etc., could in some ways be seen as rather Machiavellian and not unlike the approach advocated by Stephen Potter, but readers lapped it up. So far, it has sold over 30 million copies worldwide, is one of *the* best-selling books, and is still high on *Time* Magazine's list of the 100 most influential books of all time. Carnegie struck me as credible, and his advice resonated even more than Potter's approach as it was based on real-life experiences and key leadership figures from history. But paramount for me was that it highlighted how changing our behaviours might impact on ourselves and also others in a highly positive way. It was a win-win! I wanted to know more, and that famous book helped set me on the road to a career in psychology where I was able to help others enhance their interpersonal influence and to great effect. Reflective Goal Setting helps us to improve how we interact with others and manage the impression we create but aims to do this in a self-aware way that ties in with our values. It also encourages us to consider others and their views and responses to our goals throughout the process.

Moment for Reflection
Have you ever read something that resulted in a light bulb moment for you regarding your personal development?
What was the key message that you took away from that?

"I Got My Promotion This Week Because of You!"

Fast forward some years later to the late 1980s and I was a young and relatively recent and inexperienced graduate of psychology teaching a part-time evening class of adult students at a college in Manchester, UK. The syllabus was covering many classic and contemporary theories of psychology and in one session, the focus was on theories of non-verbal communication. The following week a woman arrived back to the class, smiled, and exclaimed, 'I got my promotion this week because of you!'. I was a tad confused until she explained that following our session on body language, she had taken the theory of mirroring and applied it to her annual performance appraisal review (e.g., Chartrand & Bargh, 1999). In its natural and spontaneous form, mirroring is a behavioural act that suggests we are empathising with someone else. It is subconscious mimicry of others' gestures, posture, and words. However, it can be engaged in deliberately—as in the example—to build rapport for influencing others. At an unconscious level, it's a sign we are in tune and in sync, think about when babies connect with their parents or caregivers (e.g., Gergely & Watson, 1996). When done consciously, it can be powerful, but can also be clumsy and/or manipulative. Mirroring is something close friends, family, and lovers do naturally, and it shows trust, comfort, and rapport. It's not just that people like to see themselves mirrored back, it communicates an eagerness to genuinely connect and understand another person. Several students of mine have set this as a goal over the years with great results.

In the example, my student had mirrored her boss's behaviour throughout and—despite having unsuccessfully applied for a promotion on several occasions—this time it had worked! No one can be sure whether the mirroring behaviour was the factor that secured it, but she was convinced that somehow it was. Her boss may have been unaware of it, as it may have only influenced him subconsciously. However, she was showing faith in the use of psychological theory in practice. The apparent power I had garnered as I shared this psychological nugget did concern me, however. It made me cautious of sharing ideas and sources not backed by solid research. It motivated me to carry out my own investigations of psychological phenomena so that I could offer evidence-based solutions and advice to others to enhance their working lives and practice.

I also realised that people gained confidence from having interpersonal techniques up their sleeve—as with any other skill—and were motivated to try them out. The outcomes could also be beneficial and far reaching. Reflective Goal Setting is about enhancing peoples' confidence for using these kinds of skills supported by strong psychological theory.

> **Moment for Reflection**
> Have you ever been conscious of others mirroring you, or you mirroring them in return?
> If you have children, you might remember back to when they were babies and they mirrored you smiling, for example.
> Next time you go out for a coffee with a friend or colleague try a little experiment, pick up your cup, and see how long it takes them to do the same? (Don't do it with your phone though, that ruins communication!)
> If you had to pick some aspect of non-verbal communication to work on for yourself, what would it be and why?

"You Need to be More Assertive Brian!"

In another example, as a trainer running a project management course in a UK-based FMCG company back in the early 1990s, I was working with a product development team in the R&D division. The team had Brian at the helm. Brian had constantly received feedback from his team that he 'needed to be more assertive,' but he was not sure what this meant in practice. He was rather soft hearted and did not find it that easy to lead from the front, having been most likely promoted due to his brilliance as a scientist, rather than as a leader. He wanted to do right by his team but felt that to change his behaviour in this way was overwhelming. He didn't know where to start.

We gave his team some training on how to give more constructive and helpful feedback. When we drilled down into the specifics to enable Brian to set an effective development goal, it became clear that they felt he did not effectively manage the more loquacious members of the team who stole all the airtime in meetings. Once they gave the more specific feedback, with honesty, and specific illustrated examples, Brain was able to set himself a clear and specific goal. This made me realise that the transfer of learning may fail because we provide or seek feedback in generalities, and effective goal setting requires specifics. Reflective Goal Setting requires us to use features of Goal Setting Theory (Locke & Latham, 1990: see Chap. 3) to work on specifying our goals and associated behaviours.

> **Moment to Reflect**
> Have you ever received a piece of feedback that surprised you, or confused you, and you didn't know where to start?
> Did you seek out clarification or let it go?
> How do you usually go about giving feedback to others?

The Forced Silence of the Extrovert

When I started working as a university lecturer, I grasped and created every opportunity I could to develop skills-based courses for managers and leaders. I wanted to help them become more effective influencers, better communicators, happier self-managers, and self-regulators. Teaching personal development sessions to groups of MBA students alerted me to how 'tough' the supposed 'softer' skills are to acquire and transfer into the workplace and I wanted to find out why.

Let's look at an example.

A manager on my MBA 'Professional Development' course had decided to set a goal to reduce her extroverted behaviour as part of a personal development coursework assignment. Prior feedback from her team had alerted her to the fact that she took up most of the airtime in meetings and spoke over people in her enthusiasm to get her point of view across (Maybe a job for Brian!). She had completed a couple of personality tests and felt that they represented her rather well. She recognised that she was extroverted in nature, tended to externalise things, and that she was uncomfortable with long silences—even short ones! She wanted to curb this and went away to put her goal of reducing her need to talk into action. However, her chosen strategy was to just stop talking! She went into meetings and stopped contributing (unless she had a clear item on the agenda that could not be dealt with by anyone else). She had focused on the wrong specifics!

How do you expect her colleagues responded to her goal attempts? Well, they were understandably unsettled by her sudden apparent lack of energy and contribution and fed back to her that they thought she was either ill or being dismissive. She reported back to me that her goal had failed due to her team's bad reception to the changes she had made. She concluded that she may as well go back to contributing in her usual way, as that seemed to be what they wanted from her after all.

Not entirely.

I invited her to reflect on why this was *not* the case. With some coaching and the right questions posed, she came up with the following reflections:

- She realised that in many cases people *did* rely on her to contribute on their behalf and that she had got into the habit of this.
- But she had not considered her *consistent story* with extroversion and talking a lot. When she did, she realised that this was also an issue for her at school and in all her previous job roles.
- She had not *brainstormed potential goals* and examined *specifically* where she should target her efforts.
- She had not *visualised* the impact that 'not speaking' would have on others in her team.
- She had failed to observe *role models* she worked with who contributed fully, but equally in meetings.
- She had not *compared her current behaviours with an ideal* to gain calibration and authenticity.
- She had not sought out any *tips for best practice*.
- She had not considered a *range of measurement indictors* to monitor her progress.
- She had not *written out her goal* in full.
- She had just gone and put what she felt was the *only solution* into practice like a loose cannon—and just stopped talking!
- She had put the goal *into practice* twice, got a bad reception and so gave up!

Therefore, it was no surprise that people were wrong-footed by her approach to their initial piece of feedback.

This example alerted me to many key important aspects of personal development goal setting that subsequently became part of the model and will be outlined in later chapters. One essential requirement was choosing a suitable way of documenting and monitoring goal attempts and reflecting on the process as it evolves. I considered that written reflection might bring about the realisation that goal attempts fail for several reasons and that some of those might be due to our own behaviour and poor choice of techniques—hence on-going written reflection is a key component of Reflective Goal Setting.

> **Moment for Reflection**
> What typically happens when you make attempts at some aspect of behaviour change?
> What responses have you had from others?
> Using our extroverted goal setter as an example, what could you try to do to bring about more effective behaviour change?

So, How Do These Examples Lead to the Model?

The illustrations shared highlight the types of skills which are the focus of this book—that is, the softer skills, and interpersonal skills in particular—crucial in all walks of life, and especially at work. As a response to my experiences, and the theories and models I was encountering about the challenges of soft skills development, I started to seek out more creative approaches to help people develop these skills and put them into practice effectively. I accessed a stored memory from my days of investigating teacher stress for my doctoral research. In teacher training and education, reflective journaling is frequently used as a way for trainees to reflect on their practice. However, I couldn't find any examples of this approach in business and management education. Nor did there appear to be any real use of goals as part of the process. So, I brought together Goal Setting Theory with writing about our goals and that's how Reflective Goal Setting started. This added feature of an on-going written reflective diary was to some extent inspired by the work of James Pennebaker on trauma narration (e.g., Pennebaker, 1997). More on this in Chap. 4.

Since 2002, my work with Reflective Goal Setting has shown that it can be applied to any behaviour we may wish to develop and change, especially those related softer skills that are believed to be lacking in rigour or objective measurement. If coupled with on-going and in-depth written reflection, success can be achieved. The impact of writing goals down has been proven to be a powerful lever for personal change and growth in other recent studies, as well as my own (e.g., Morisano et al., 2010; Schippers et al., 2020, 2015). This will be outlined in more depth in Chap. 3.

Following the creation of this approach with managers and leaders, I started to use it with undergraduate final year students on a course entitled—Advanced Interpersonal Skills. Following an internship year, these students worked with me to develop their leadership skills, employability, self-management, and communication. They became familiar with crucial psychological theories in these areas—from my classroom teaching, and their own wider research, and used their new knowledge to set suitable goals. I knew I was onto something when students started to tell me that the process of Reflective Goal Setting impacted on their lives in general, their relationships, academic studies, and job success.

SUMMARY

- Business school students will typically find themselves in managerial roles and/or as leaders in the future. This is not exclusive to business students, however, as students from any academic discipline will enter the world of work and be required to display quality 'soft' skills, especially those relating to face-to-face communication with others and a desire and capacity for personal development.
- In addition, leaders require a whole host of soft and interpersonal skills due to the pressures to manage a variety of complex people issues. These behaviours can have a significant impact on the well-being and satisfaction of employees. But evidence suggests that these soft skills are lacking.
- Being able to set impactful goals is an essential leader skill, both in terms of a leader's own personal development and for supporting the development of others. Contemporary leaders are expected to support and coach others and to set and meet their respective goals via the development of key skills.
- Reflective Goal Setting is a five-stage model that is designed to support personal and leader development. To get an idea of some of its key features, have a go at the checklist in Appendix 1. How many can you say you already engage in at this moment in time? You can come back to it again at the end of the book.

Appendix 1

Some Key Reflective Goal Setting Behaviours: How Many Can You Tick Off as Being Things You Do Already?

When setting goals:

I first identify relevant self-awareness activities.
I begin by identifying my core values.
I first gather feedback from trusted sources and evaluate the feedback.
I try to consider the impact they will have on others (e.g., friends, family, manager, team).
I ask for feedback on my goal choice wherever possible (e.g., from friends, family, mentors).
I choose a goal that is relevant and important to me personally.
I identify the effective behaviours I want to achieve.
I visualise myself behaving more effectively in my goal-related scenario.
I first identify best practice and/or role models to guide me.
I write them down with a detailed goal plan.
I identify appropriate measurement criteria to monitor my progress.
I identify relevant techniques and approaches to apply.
I seek out 'practice grounds' to test out my goal.
I consolidate any learning into my self-awareness.
I feel equipped to deal with goal setbacks that may occur.

Also, a couple of general related questions:

I enjoy setting goals for myself.
I have kept diaries in the past.
I am usually confident that I will achieve my goals.

And one last question, on a scale of 1–10 (1 being not at all and 10 being fully), how confident do you feel at this moment regarding your ability to set achievable goals using Reflective Goal Setting?

REFERENCES

Chartrand, T. L., & Bargh, J. A. (1999). The chameleon effect: The perception–behavior link and social interaction. *Journal of Personality and Social Psychology, 76*(6), 893.

Clarke, M. (2017). Building employability through graduate development programmes: A case study in an Australian public sector organisation. *Personnel Review, 46*(4), 792–808.

Crossman, J. E., & Clarke, M. (2010). International experience and graduate employability: Stakeholder perceptions on the connection. *Higher Education, 59*(5), 599–613.

Gergely, G., & Watson, J. S. (1996). The social biofeedback theory of parental affect-mirroring: The development of emotional self-awareness and self-control in infancy. *International Journal of Psycho-Analysis, 77,* 1181–1212.

Goffee, R., & Jones, G. 2000. Why should anyone be led by you?. *Harvard Business Review.*

Haselberger, D., Oberheumer, P., Perez, E., Cinque, M., & Capasso, D. 2012. Mediating soft skills at higher education institutions, handbook of ModEs project, lifelong learning programme. *European Union,* pp. 1–133.

Hunt, J. W., & Baruch, Y. (2003). Developing top managers: The impact of interpersonal skills training. *Journal of Management Development, 22*(8), 729–752.

Klein, C., DeRouin, R. E., & Salas, E. (2006). Uncovering workplace interpersonal skills: A review, framework, and research agenda. In G. P. Hodgkinson & J. K. Ford (Eds.), *International review of industrial and organizational psychology 2006* (pp. 79–126). Wiley Publishing.

Locke, E. A., & Latham, G. P. (Eds.). (2013). *New developments in goal setting and task performance.* Routledge and Taylor & Francis Group.

Morisano, D., Hirsh, J. B., Peterson, J. B., Pihl, R. O., & Shore, B. M. (2010). Setting, elaborating, and reflecting on personal goals improves academic performance. *Journal of Applied Psychology, 95*(2), 255.

Moursched, M., Farrell, D., & Barton, D. (2012). *Education to employment: Designing a system that works.* McKinsey Centre for Government, McKinsey and Company. Retrieved July 5, 2016, from http://mckinseyonsociety.com/downloads/reports/education/education-to-employment_final.pdf

Pennebaker, J. W. (1997). Writing about emotional experiences as a therapeutic process. *Psychological Science, 8*(3), 162–166.

Robles, M. M. (2012). Executive perceptions of the top 10 soft skills needed in today's workplace. *Business Communication Quarterly, 75*(4), 453–465.

Schippers, M. C., Morisano, D., Locke, E. A., Scheepers, A. W., Latham, G. P., & de Jong, E. M. (2020). Writing about personal goals and plans regardless of goal type boosts academic performance. *Contemporary Educational Psychology, 60,* 101823.

Schippers, M. C., Scheepers, A. W., & Peterson, J. B. (2015). A scalable goal-setting intervention closes both the gender and ethnic minority achievement gap. *Palgrave Communications, 1*(1), 1–12.

Schön, D. A. (1983). *The reflective practitioner: How professionals think in action.* Basic Books. (Reprinted in 1995).

CHAPTER 2

Reflective Goal Setting and the Transfer of Learning

How Can the Model Help Us Transfer Learning for Personal and Leader Development?

Abstract Reflective Goal Setting is predominantly a framework to support the transfer of learning for personal and leader development, especially for the development of softer skills. This chapter does not intend to provide an extensive review of the transfer of learning literature, but rather defines it, discusses some of the issues faced when we are dealing with adult education and personal development, and shows how Reflective Goal Setting can support learning transfer in this space.

Keywords Transfer of learning • Andragogy • Pedagogy • Transformative learning • Reflective practice • Evaluation

Introduction

The Reluctant Delegator

Faridah had been on many training courses. She had recently attended '*How to be an effective leader*' as part of her MSc programme at a business school, and within that had been taught how to delegate. She had the notes—they took you through key models for delegation—stage by stage. Whilst in the classroom she felt full of enthusiasm and the slides, self-assessment questionnaires, theoretical models, and online activities provided by her tutors made it seem so easy. She had even made a verbal commitment to delegate more at the end of the session when the tutor went around the group asking them for the one thing they were going to take away and put into practice. Her intentions were good. She could even talk about the approach she would take when she went home and chatted to her partner about the learning experience. She could see the rationale for delegating, for example, and understood that it could be both beneficial for her as the manager, and for members of her team. However, as soon as she returned to her workplace, as usual, things always seemed to get in the way of those good intentions. She still took on far too much and failed to give anything away. She felt under pressure, which quickly turned to stress, and though it seemed as good a time as any to spread the load, she just continued in her old ways. She was still aware that something had to change, but still wasn't sure how to put her learning into practice.

Moment for Reflection

What do you think might be getting in the way of Faridah's attempts to transfer her learning from the training course back to work?

How have you fared when transferring learning from training courses you have attended?

What has helped or hindered in that transfer of skills for impact away from the training?

"What's shocking is that although there's a lot of literature about what is needed to make long lasting behaviour change a lot of people haven't taken it seriously....they spray employees with the concept and pray that it will make a difference."—Murray Dalziel

My career as a university teacher and researcher has been spent in business schools working with undergraduate and postgraduate students eager to secure interesting and worthwhile careers and achieve future leadership roles within their preferred organisations. Also, I have been employed to work with a multitude of managers and leaders, like Faridah, on programmes commissioned by their companies with a view to enhancing their leadership, self-insight, and add value to their businesses. This variety of experiences has shed light on the challenges affecting the successful transfer of learning.

From an organisational point of view, the largest proportion of organizational training budgets are allocated to leadership training, yet, despite the major investment of time and money, practical application beyond the training room is not guaranteed (Lacerenza et al., 2017; Beer et al., 2016). One possible reason is that the transfer of learning is frequently downplayed and unsupported by organisations who make limited efforts to ensure learning transfers across to improve job performance. However, many critics believe a key responsibility lies with those who provide business and management education to both undergraduate students and managers and leaders. For example, many scholars have questioned the ability of business schools to equip their students for a successful professional career (Bennis & O'Toole, 2005). Employers frequently express satisfaction with the 'hard' functional or technical skills of business graduates (e.g., accounting), but dissatisfaction with crucial soft skills (Datar et al., 2010). A commonality of these criticisms is that, despite much academic literature on the topic, little attention is paid to how educators can deliver educational experiences which optimise learning transfer of these types of skills. An emphasis on the structural and theoretical aspects of a course curriculum dominates, with insufficient focus on how learning will be put to practical use. For example, traditional approaches to soft skills development for students and corporate clients include such features as 'chalk and talk' about theories and frameworks, followed by role-play of specific interpersonal situations (e.g., give a short presentation in front of other trainees) with feedback (e.g., watching recordings of a presentation with course mates followed by debrief) (Salas et al., 2009). But this is no substitute for real-life application and insufficient attempts are made to create the means to apply these skills beyond the classroom. Once the feedback 'happy sheets' are completed, a trainer's responsibility typically ends, and course attendees and their organisations are on their own. The same applies to business school graduates entering the world of work.

Another factor may be an educators' lack of sensitivity to the requirements of business school university undergraduates: that is, are these 18–23-year-old learners in *early* adulthood (Brookfield, 2015) or *emerging* adulthood? (Arnett, 2000). Emerging adulthood is associated with certain developmental challenges, including identity exploration. As adults, we need to process our experiences, become self-aware, and acquire professional and social skills—requiring reflective processes and critical thinking (Raikou & Filippidi, 2019). Business school education should be providing opportunities for learners to develop skills of reflection at this crucial intermediate life stage as a foundation to other learning requirements at university and when they enter the workplace.

Contemporary workplaces exist in a constantly changing business landscape requiring greater flexibility and adaptability. In return, they expect flexible and adaptable employees who can compete internationally, use information technology efficiently, react speedily to changes to their work environments, and show self-initiative (Greenhaus & Kossek, 2014; Van der Heijden et al., 2008). Careers are also changing and are more typically composed of horizontal career progression, multiple job roles, global mobility, and portfolio working (Grant-Smith & McDonald, 2018). Consequently, business graduates will face a diverse range of working contexts and will be required to transfer skills and knowledge more frequently. They need to be confident in their ability to manage transitions and upskill when required. Reflective Goal Setting can support them in this transfer of learning at these crucial career stages.

What Do We Mean by the Transfer of Learning?

Perkins and Salomon (1992) suggest that transfer of learning occurs when learning in a particular context enhances (positive transfer) or undermines (negative transfer) some form of a related performance in a different context. Such transfer includes what they term *near* transfer (to closely related contexts and performances) and *far* transfer (to different contexts and performances). They suggest that two key mechanisms lead to learning transfer: *reflexive* transfer involves applying well-practiced routines to conditions like those in the learning context (e.g., answering a question on a topic in an exam that you have revised at home). On the other hand, *mindful* transfer involves the deliberate, effortful abstraction and a search for connections in a range of contexts and scenarios, which might be removed from the original (e.g., applying team working skills in a new project team, based on things you learnt in a sports context). Conventional educational practices often fail to establish the conditions either for reflexive or mindful transfer largely due to their design. For example, the way information is transmitted in classrooms (e.g., course notes and folders with lots of theory, online tasks, and activities) differs from the ultimate contexts of application (in the home, on the job, within complex tasks).

Perkins and Salomon further suggest three sets of work factors that can influence the post-training transfer of soft skills—that is, job-related, social support, and factors related to the organisational facilitation of learning. Let's look back at the case of Faridah. There may have been a lack of trained staff available to take on her job tasks, she may have had a lack of support from her team, pressure from her line manager to do it herself, no coaching or mentoring in place, etc. However, it could also be related to the training itself. There could have been insufficient planning for learning transfer and evaluation following the delivery of the programme. Plus, Faridah's own character might be holding her back: she may prefer to just do it herself; she might struggle to trust others, she possibly feels threatened that someone might do it better than her, etc. Transfer of learning is complex and multifaceted, but it helps to gain an understanding of how adults learn.

What Do We Know About How Adults Learn?

Adults learn differently to children. Knowles (1980) was one of the first to differentiate between the two and suggested that, unlike children, adults are intrinsically motivated, self-directed learners. They are mature, bring with them resources and experiences, and they are task, problem, and life centred. Knowles argued that these inherent differences necessitated a different learning model for adults than for children; one that is process rather than content driven, which is particularly beneficial to managers and leaders in educational settings (Bernon & Mena, 2013). To accept what he termed 'andragogy', (originally defined by Kapp, 1833) requires a shift in thinking away from the more pedagogical assumption that education typically concerns the transition of knowledge, to one of knowledge application and implementation. Unfortunately, andragogy did not rise to be the grand theory of adult learning initially predicted, critiqued for its elusive operational definitions, lack of clarity of application, and its failure to measure the effectiveness of knowledge acquisition in practical terms (Taylor & Laros, 2014). However, as we still talk about pedagogy in university settings, this may limit the development of more innovative teaching and learning approaches for adult learners.

Let's go back to Faridah's issue with the transfer of learning. There are many general definitions of learning available, but they typically involve some statement around a relatively permanent change in behaviour due to our experiences. Learning is something that we cannot assume has taken place unless we see evidence of it, so in many ways it is hypothetical, as we can only infer learning from someone's behaviour but learning itself cannot be observed directly. In Faridah's case, she may have believed she had learned how to delegate due to all the content provided on her course and in class tests, etc., but this was not subsequently evident in her behaviour. This suggests that she may have, albeit temporarily, learnt the theory behind delegation but had not been able or willing to show that learning in action.

In another scenario, a temporary change in behaviour may take place, and we can assume the presence of learning transfer, but this could be due to other factors, such as close and short-term managerial supervision of learned behaviours following training. So, this might not be claimed as evidence of successful transfer. This makes learning about soft skills theories and frameworks in the classroom without consideration of further transfer, a rather pointless exercise. One approach is to compare our new ideal behaviour with that of our behaviour before the training and this is a crucial component of Reflective Goal Setting and will be covered in later chapters.

The transfer of skills and knowledge is a complex area of learning theory which lacks sufficient empirical analysis, despite there being many different theories (Hakel & Halpern, 2005). More traditional approaches are concerned with cognitive processing and outputs transferred out of the original learning situation (Mestre, 2005). These tend to be narrow in their focus on repetition of prior knowledge. However, these approaches give little allowance for learners to revise and trial new ways to adapt earlier learning in the new context. So, they are perhaps effective for the transfer of technical skills, but not for those softer in nature, nor do they help us prepare for future learning and adapting to novel circumstances (Bransford & Schwartz, 1999). Reflective Goal Setting aims to develop this ability to prepare for future and on-going learning and will be discussed in depth in Part 2.

Building on andragogy, 'Transformative Learning Theory' made its mark on the field of adult education in the early 1990s and was a key influence on my thinking around Reflective Goal setting. Mezirow (1978–2009) is the main theorist in this area, defining Transformative Learning as "the process of effecting a change in a frame of reference" and viewing transformation "as a qualitative change of cognitive perspective," emphasising the development of autonomous thinking (cited Tosey et al., 2005, p. 141). Some see Mezirow's approach as strongly cognitive, but most agree it is an appropriate theoretical framework for addressing adult learning that can be considered in both formal and informal contexts. He further defines learning to be the process of "using a prior interpretation to construe a new or revised interpretation of the meaning of one's experience to guide future action" (cited Thomas, 2012, p. 556). For adults, this involves bringing their life experiences to the learning context and learning to critically think for themselves. Meaning making and critical reflection are therefore two important aspects of Transformative Learning. According to Taylor and Laros (2014), this emphasis on critical reflection is one of the key characteristics that distinguishes Transformative Learning from other adult learning theories.

The field of Transformative Learning is still developing, especially in leadership and management education, but the increase in critical literature and studies evaluating it in practice (Hodge, 2011; Cox, 2015) shows that it is now firmly established as an influential adult learning theory. We will learn more about reflection in Chap. 4, as meaning making and critical reflection feature heavily in Reflective Goal Setting.

What Are the Usual Approaches for Evaluating the Transfer of Learning in Organisations?

It is important that we can evaluate the impact of business and management education and the transfer of learning, especially in organisational contexts. Part 3 will illustrate impact from the use of Reflective Goal Setting on several skill areas, and Chap. 11 especially will examine its impact in three organisational contexts. There are several evaluation frameworks that have emerged over the years. For example, the Kirkpatrick model (e.g., 1996) is based on four stages or levels of evaluation—reaction, learning, behaviour, and results. It ultimately concentrates on impact of education in economic terms or 'Return on Investment' (ROI). Many have found this model outdated and limiting, and it is less effective when it comes to evaluating the impact of less quantifiable softer skills. However, it is important that organisations see the impact from their investment in adult education.

Eiter and Halperin (2010) surveyed business clients and providers of executive education programmes regarding their suggested evaluative frameworks for assessing the transfer of learning from educational settings to the workplace. These frameworks fell broadly into the following five measures:

- **Process measure**—mapping numbers of participants on a course against the cost.
- **Satisfaction measures**—taken at the end of a programme ('happy' sheets).
- **Progress measures**—subsequent promotions, layoffs.
- **Usage measures**—specific examples of how and where programme content/frameworks had been used in the workplace.
- **Business value measures**—demonstrating take up of ideas and any embedding within the organisation.

They conclude that recent years have seen a shift from single quantitative measures such as ROI towards multiple measures of impact that use both qualitative and quantitative measures. They believe clients are looking for "tangible evidence of program impact" (Eiter & Halperin, 2010, p. 19). This reinforces the need for organisational buy-in to the process of learning transfer and evaluation. Choy (2009, p. 80) argues that "learning needs to be acknowledged, supported, and formally valued as organisational capability for it to be transformative and effective." Haskins and Clawson (2006) suggest institutional support could be provided in the form of coaching relationships in the workplace once participants have returned to their organisation. They believe this could aid the transfer of learning and ensure its '*stickiness*'. Choy (2009, p. 82) further argues that the reflective elements of transformational learning are crucial: "reflective thinking, reflective discourses and reasoning that challenged them to change their perspectives... [led to]...new perspectives [that] were more inclusive, discriminating, open and reflective, and acceptable to their colleagues."

One of the main points about evaluating the transfer of learning is the timing of evaluations. Several scholars argue it should occur at three points, that is, pre-course evaluation, immediately after and sometime later (Dawson, 1995). From my experience, this approach tends to run out of steam. A key issue is that though adult learners have the experiences to reflect and build on, they are typically time poor and find it difficult to make the time or space to reflect and develop further understanding

(Bernon & Mena, 2013). Therefore, considering what the adult learner brings to the learning experience and building in time for critical reflection are important elements of any evaluative framework at this level.

How Does Reflective Goal Setting Improve the Transfer of Learning?

Reflective Goal Setting builds impact considerations into the process and equips learners with the goal-setting skills to transfer their learning beyond the classroom and the critical reflective skills to monitor and evaluate their own personal development progress. It also provides a framework that managers, leaders, coaches, and mentors can use to support goal setters during and after that process. But essentially, it places the goal setter at the centre of their own evaluation of learning transfer and progress.

Summary

- The transfer of learning from approaches to personal development and soft skills acquisition and learning is challenging due to the nature of the skills themselves, an individual's lack of know-how, factors in the organisation, and the lack of objectivity of measurement.
- A focus on pedagogy relies too heavily on curriculum development, and we need to focus on adult learning approaches, such as Transformative Learning.
- For personal development to take place, learners need to be more involved in their learning, bringing in their experiences.
- Time needs to be built in for critical reflection whilst applying learning and goal setting.
- Reflective Goal Setting offers a longitudinal framework for personal development and soft skills education and learning to facilitate ongoing skill development.

References

Arnett, J. J. (2000). Emerging adulthood: A theory of development from the late teens through the twenties. *American Psychologist, 55*, 469–480.

Beer, M., Finnström, M., & Schrader, D. (2016). Why leadership training fails— and what to do about it. *Harvard Business Review, 94*(10), 50–57.

Bennis, W. G., & O'Toole, J. (2005). How business schools have lost their way. *Harvard Business Review, 83*(5), 96–104.

Bernon, M., & Mena, C. (2013). The evolution of customised executive education in supply chain management. *Supply Chain Management: An International Journal, 18*, 440–453.

Bransford, J. D., & Schwartz, D. L. (1999). Chapter 3: Rethinking transfer: A simple proposal with multiple implications. *Review of Research in Education, 24*(1), 61–100.

Brookfield, S. D. (2015). *The skillful teacher: On technique, trust, and responsiveness in the classroom.* Jossey-Bass.

Choy, S. (2009). Transformational learning in the workplace. *Journal of Transformative Education, 7*(1), 65–84.

Cox, E. (2015). Coaching and adult learning: Theory and practice. *New Directions for Adult and Continuing Education, 2015*(148), 27–38.

Datar, S. M., Garvin, D. A., Cullen, P. G., & Cullen, P. (2010). *Rethinking the MBA: Business education at a crossroads.* Harvard Business Press.

Dawson, R. (1995). Fill this in before you go: Under-utilized evaluation sheets. *Journal of European Industrial Training, 19*(2), 3–7.

Eiter, M., & Halperin, R. (2010). Investigating emerging practices in executive program evaluation. *UNICON research paper.*

Grant-Smith, D., & McDonald, P. (2018). Ubiquitous yet ambiguous: An integrative review of unpaid work. *International Journal of Management Reviews, 20*(2), 559–578.

Greenhaus, J. H., & Kossek, E. E. (2014). The contemporary career: A work–home perspective. *Annual Review of Organizational Psychology and Organizational Behavior, 1*(1), 361–388.

Hakel, M., & Halpern, D. F. (2005). How far can transfer go? Making transfer happen across physical, temporal, and conceptual space. In *Transfer of learning from a modern multidisciplinary perspective* (pp. 357–370). Information Age Publishing.

Haskins, M. E., & Clawson, J. G. (2006). Making it sticky: How to facilitate the transfer of executive education experiences back to the workplace. *Journal of Management Development, 25*, 850–869.

Hodge, S. (2011). Learning to manage: Transformative outcomes of competency-based training. *Australian Journal of Adult Learning, 51*(3), 498–517.

Kapp, A. (1833). *Platon's Erziehungslehre, als Pädagogik für die Einzelnen und als Staatspädagogik. Oder dessen praktische Philosophie aus den Quellen dargestellt von Alexander Kapp.* F. Essmann.

Kirkpatrick, D. (1996). *Great ideas revisited.* Techniques for evaluating training programs. Revisiting Kirkpatri.

Knowles, M. (1980). *The modern practice of adult education: From pedagogy to andragogy* (2nd ed.). Cambridge Books.

Lacerenza, C. N., Reyes, D. L., Marlow, S. L., Joseph, D. L., & Salas, E. (2017). Leadership training design, delivery, and implementation: A meta-analysis. *Journal of Applied Psychology, 102*(12), 1686.

Mestre, J. (2005, September). Is transfer ubiquitous or rare? New paradigms for studying transfer. In *AIP Conference Proceedings* (Vol. 790, No. 1, pp. 3–6). American Institute of Physics.

Perkins, D. N., & Salomon, G. (1992). Transfer of learning. *International Encyclopedia of Education, 2*, 6452–6457.

Raikou, N., & Filippidi, A. (2019). Emerging adulthood and university teachers' education. In *Proceedings of the 11th Panhellenic Conference of Hellenic Educational Society (108–116)*. DPE University of Patras (in Greek).

Salas, E., Wildman, J. L., & Piccolo, R. F. (2009). Using simulation-based training to enhance management education. *Academy of Management Learning & Education, 8*(4), 559–573.

Taylor, E. W., & Laros, A. (2014). Researching the practice of fostering transformative learning: Lessons learned from the study of andragogy. *Journal of Transformative Education, 12*(2), 134–147.

Thomas, P. L. (2012). Charge nurses as front-line leaders: Development through transformative learning. *The Journal of Continuing Education in Nursing, 43*(2), 67–74.

Tosey, P., Mathison, J., & Michelli, D. (2005). Mapping transformative learning: The potential of neuro-linguistic programming. *Journal of Transformative Education, 3*(2), 140–167.

Van Der Heijden, B. I., Schalk, R., & Van Veldhoven, M. J. (2008). Ageing and careers: European research on long-term career development and early retirement. *Career Development International, 13*, 85–94.

CHAPTER 3

Reflective Goal Setting, Goal Setting Theory, and the Importance of Writing About Goals

What Do We Know About The Impact Of Writing About Our Goals?

Abstract This chapter focuses on a fundamental feature of Reflective Goal Setting—writing about our goals. It will firstly show how the model has been influenced by other approaches to goal setting, especially the Goal Setting Theory (GST) of Edwin Locke and Gary Latham. The chapter is not intended to be an extensive literature review of the field but will outline the main features of Goal Setting Theory and show how Reflective Goal Setting builds on that. Secondly, current thinking on the importance of writing in detail about our goals will be presented.

Keywords Goal Setting Theory • Self-regulation • Self-efficacy • Writing about goals

© The Author(s), under exclusive license to Springer Nature Switzerland AG 2022
C. J. Travers, *Reflective Goal Setting*,
https://doi.org/10.1007/978-3-030-99228-6_3

Introduction

Two Men, Two Goals, One Six-Pack

Senior leaders from a UK-based wealth management company were attending a leader development programme run by myself and colleagues at my Business School. The topic of my day was stress, resilience, and well-being, and at the end of the session, group members were invited to share their goal ideas for well-being enhancement. Two delegates expressed their desire to develop their physical fitness by regular attendance at the gym—as both a distraction from incessant work, and to improve their overall energy levels and work-life balance. Both were experiencing increasing pressures in their leader roles, leaving little time for their health and wellbeing. They reported that they were feeling sluggish and tired, putting on weight, and felt increasingly out of control. Neglect of their health was taking its toll and they believed a fitness goal might be the way forward. So, they finished the workshop verbally committing to a goal to attend their local gym three times a week. Their task was to go away and write out their goal in full and document their progress in a reflective diary.

During a follow-up session with the group, three months later, delegates were asked to provide feedback on their goal progress. One of the gym-goal-guys was visibly more toned and slim and seemed 'brighter eyed.' He explained that he had lost a stone in weight and had exceeeded his expectations—managing to go to the gym on average five times a week. He was thrilled with his progress and said he felt so much more in control of the stress and pressure of his job. The gym was providing much needed detachment from work and had put a bounce in his step at home. He was feeling more able to knock a ball around with his sons too. The gym had become a good habit and part of his weekly routine and work seemed more manageable consequently.

Our other gym-goal-guy looked on, clearly surprised, and displayed a touch of envy. He went on to lament some weight gain since our last session and admitted that he had only managed to go to the gym once a week for the first two weeks and then nothing since. He'd struggled to make time and get back into the swing of it. He reported still feeling tired and overwhelmed with work.

(continued)

So, I asked them to explore why there might have been such a different outcome—one goal setter successful to the point of transcendence and one who had failed to the point of despondence.

Though this one illustration would not make its way into a top research journal, the main conclusion drawn matched many I have witnessed over the years of using Reflective Goal Setting and supports findings from other researchers in the field.

One gym-goal-guy had gone away and taken the time to write down his goal in specific detail—what exactly he was going to do, and why, how he was going to do it, and when, what types of support he might need, how he was going to measure his progress (as well as the 'objective' measure of number of times he attended the gym, any weight lost, he anticipated potential increased sense of accomplishment, others' positive reactions, more patience, better sleep patterns, etc.).

The other gym-goal-guy reported that on leaving the training room he couldn't be bothered to write the goal down and thought mentioning it to his wife that evening was enough.

This is just one example of the impact of writing goals down.

Which one of our senior managers do you think had written their goal down in detail—Mr Gym Transcendence or Mr Gym Despondence?

"By recording your dreams and goals on paper, you set in motion the process of becoming the person you most want to be. Put your future in good hands—your own."—Mark Victor Hansen

So, What Are Goals and Why Are They Important?

The Oxford English Dictionary defines a goal as "The object to which effort or ambition is directed; the destination of a (more or less laborious) journey. ... An end or result towards which behaviour is consciously or unconsciously directed." Conscious goals are those which when actively pursued can make the difference between effective performance, success, happiness, and wellbeing in our work and non-work lives. Goal setting research has usually focused on conscious goals. Though a key model of motivation and behavioural change, in its classic form Goal Setting Theory is limited as a mechanism for the development of softer and interpersonal skills. This is possibly because by and large, much of our behaviour is directed and motivated by goals outside of our conscious awareness, priming us for any given situation (Aarts & Custers, 2012).

Reflect for a moment, on how many acts you perform without a great deal of thought or how many are based around automated habit. For example, if we refer to our gym-goal-guys, one reported that following a typically hectic day at the office, he would usually arrive home and instantly pour himself a large glass of red wine and search for a snack—usually crisps—without any thought at all. Those days were becoming more frequent. Yes, that was Mr Gym-Despondence.

Unconscious priming makes it hard for us to control unhelpful behaviours and habits unless we can find ways of bringing them under our conscious control. We tend to think of habits as things like smoking, drinking alcohol, nail biting, etc. These behaviours can have an impact on our interpersonal relations, and so many reflective goal setters have chosen to work on reducing these over the years. But habitual and frequently maladaptive responses can also apply to our thoughts, feelings, and interactions with others too—that is, the 'softer' and interpersonal behaviours. For example, in the workplace, we may have certain people who 'rub us up the wrong way,' 'press our buttons,' and we may react towards them without any control and conscious thought. We may not even remember why, if we ever knew in the first place. Or, for example, we may find that we have automatic thoughts about our (in)competence as a leader which in turn creates barriers to our progress.

Reflective Goal Setting seeks to bring as much goal pursuit as possible into the conscious to differentiate between effective and non-effective goal behaviours. When we enhance our self-awareness in Stage 1 (see Chap. 5 for more detail), it helps us get to grips with how we approach goals, understand our patterns of behaviour, and identify the things that may reinforce our actions. We may also receive feedback on these automatic habits and ways of thinking and doing. For example:

> "My self-awareness work helped me identify that historically, I have found marketing meetings very frustrating and quite stressful because I struggle to control my emotions and behaviour. Reflecting on this and my patterns of behaviour in similar situations, I was able to see that these are my typical habitual reactions when I don't have a full understanding of the subject, goal, or a plan of action. This realisation has enabled me to set a suitable goal with support from my line manager and as such, I now do more preparation to enhance my knowledge and understanding of the topic before going into the meetings. This has given me a sense of optimism and has helped me to self-regulate, control my behaviour, cognitions, and emotional reactions during these meetings—like the mindfulness techniques I have read about. In my opinion, this new-found optimism provides me with the ability to cope better and, from what I perceive it has had the same effect on the Marketing Team and PR agency."

We typically think about goals as being focussed on performance outcomes and usually in the workplace or sporting arena. However, goals can be set on aspects which may eventually *lead* to that eventual performance. So, for example, we may wish to enhance our expertise or skills in a particular area and so set ourselves learning goals that may help foster good performance in the future. The aim of these types of goals is to improve one's skills or expertise by seeking information, experience, coaching, and/or training. There can also be goals for interpersonal behaviours, such as giving others information, warning others of a problem, giving others credit or thanks, and treating others with respect. There can be goals for process, such as going through six steps when meeting a prospective new customer or a complaining customer. The different types of goals can sometimes be combined. So that a person can work towards performing well in an area, while at the same time learning new skills that will make the outcomes even more successful. For example, setting a goal to improve revision technique, along with another for developing confidence in asking for help from lecturers, to gain the eventual goal of a great exam grade.

Goal Setting Theory and SMART Goals

When we think about consciously setting goals, most of us will instantly think of the much-used acronym—SMART— to help us develop our goals, targets, and objectives (Doran, 1981). From our schooldays through to our working lives, we are encouraged to make our goals specific, measurable, achievable, realistic, and time-bounded.

> **Moment for Reflection**
> Consider a goal you are currently working on—in or out of work. Would you say it was SMART?

Though we may have all heard of SMART goals, we may not know the academic origins of this simplified and much-used acronym. The relationship between conscious goals and intentions and task performance was first acknowledged and developed by the psychologist Edwin Locke in his 1968 seminal paper called "Toward a Theory of Task Motivation and Incentives." The basic premise being that an individual's conscious ideas regulate his or her actions. Locke summarised the key features of successful goal output: hard goals produce a higher level of performance/output than easy goals; specific hard goals produce a higher level of output than a goal of "do your best"; and behavioural intentions regulate choice behaviour. He also acknowledged goals as mediators of the effects of incentives on task performance. This means that monetary incentives, time limits, and knowledge of results do not affect performance level independent of the individual's goals and intentions. Also, behavioural intentions were found to mediate the effects of money and "verbal reinforcement" on choice behaviour. In addition, the goal must be important to us; we must be committed to goal attainment. Also, we must be able to obtain feedback on our goal progress so that we can make necessary adjustments on effort made and/or goal strategy. He concluded that any adequate theory of task motivation must take account of the individual's conscious goals and intentions.

By 1990, Locke formed what was to be a lifelong research partnership with Gary Latham, resulting in the first outing of their Goal Setting Theory in "A Theory of Goal Setting and Task performance." At that time, their theory was based on around 400 studies. Since that time, there has been a further 600 plus studies using Goal Setting Theory and thus its impact has expanded into many areas such as education, leadership, health promotion, among others. They have explored the use of goals within large organisations, as well as their impact on individuals. Their more recent book published in 2013, '*New Directions in task performance*' features a chapter by me on Reflective Goal Setting for personal development.

Goal Setting Theory has stood the test of time due to its validity and durability and Locke and Latham explain that its apparent stamina as a theory, is largely due to its nature as an inductive approach to theory building. They argue it is an open theory which is receptive to new discoveries. Reflective Goal Setting builds on Goal Setting Theory and to some extent contradicts some of its tenets—with their blessing!

HOW DO WE KNOW GOAL SETTING LEADS TO SUCCESS?

Quantitative methodologies have tended to dominate goal setting research and have showcased the power of goals in gaining desirable outcomes and improving performance (Latham & Locke, 2018). Goal setting is a key element of self-regulation and behaviour change. It has been shown to have unique effects on behaviour in many domains including industry, education, sports, and health care (Epton et al., 2017). Most of the research has stressed the importance of aligning a task-specific, challenging goal with a specific, desired, and related outcome. The focus on quantitative approaches has been driven by a need to measure objective changes in performance following goal setting exercises but has been insufficient for examining the detailed nature of the changes that occur, particularly when examining personal growth goals. A more qualitative approach is imperative for delving into the 'black box' of the change process (Haggis, 2002) and for gaining access to the intricacies of the transformation that has taken place (Harachi et al., 1999). Reflective Goal Setting's use of on-going written reflective diaries can help us gain such insights and some findings can be seen in Chaps. 10, 11, and 12.

Furthermore, when self-concordant goals (i.e., goals which represent a person's enduring interests and self-defining values (Sheldon et al., 2002) are combined with implementation intentions that specify the when, where, and how of goal attainment, goal progress is facilitated (Gollwitzer & Sheeran, 2006). The act of planning and strategizing is a mediator in Goal Setting Theory (Latham & Arshoff, 2015), and goal setting can set students on a path of self-regulation (Latham & Locke, 1991).

So, What Do Goal-Related Theories Tell Us About How to Set Successful Goals?

Goal setting is a critically important motivational technique, but like all management principles, its benefits depend on how skilfully it is used. Zimmerman (2008) brings together evidence from the testing of Goal Setting Theory and also features of Social Cognitive Theory (Bandura, 1986) and offers eight criteria for success when setting goals:

Goal specificity—Research suggests that broad, 'Do your best' goals do not enhance attainment in the way that specific goals can (Schunk, 1989). As I outlined in Chap. 1, my students and leaders attempting to be 'more assertive' or 'listen more effectively,' or 'be less stressed' usually failed. These were broad aims rather than goals and didn't lead to successful behavioural changes. When we set specific goals, it is easier to measure, and we focus our attention and action on these goals at the expense of others. A goal consists of two aspects: a description of an intended future state and the action(s) towards achieving that future state. We tend to quantify goal outcomes in work-settings, (e.g., number of sales made), and many people think of goals at work as being only for objective performance. But as we identified in Chap. 1, goals can exist for other actions that help foster good performance. Indeed, if we focus too much on performance, we may well encourage employees to embark on goals as tick box exercises without the underlying behaviours, attitudes, and values changing. Reflective Goal Setting works on generating the means to measure these other types of goals.

Proximity in time—To gain the most from our goal setting, we need to monitor our progress towards that goal, gain feedback, and act on it, as close in time to the activity as possible and at short time intervals as opposed to long. Reflective Goal Setting features the use of an on-going written reflective diary to enable timely reflections following a goal attempt to maximise this effect.

Degree of difficulty—Goals that are attainable but challenging are more likely to encourage personal growth. Reflective Goal Setting encourages goal setters to identify difficult goals for both personal and soft skills development. As we know, these kinds of skills are often the hardest to tackle and are by their very nature, challenging. For example, as one goal setter explained: "That 'difficult' isn't just something that stretches you a little bit. Difficult is something that you dread the thought of doing. But my word, it is rewarding when you achieve it."

Self-generated—According to Deci and Ryan's (1985) Self-Determination Theory, goals that are self-generated are likely to result in greater commitment, compared to goals that are set for us by others, if they are realistic. Locke and Latham (2002) suggest that goals that are set by, or negotiated with, others can be accepted, and committed to, if we understand and buy in to the rationale behind them. Naturally, there will be times when goal setters need guidance, and Reflective Goal Setting provides a framework to structure the approach to setting goals that shows how to obtain the subject-specific guidance needed.

Congruence between our goals and those of others—Building on the previous point, if we can align our goals with significant others in our lives, we are less likely to have our goals challenged and will therefore have greater success. Reflective Goal Setting encourages goal setters to gain feedback on goals from others and consider their needs.

Level of conscious awareness—Many of our behaviours and actions are carried out with little conscious thought and in an automatic way. This may lead to efficiency when we have a well-honed skill, but when setting goals on new skills or areas requiring development, our conscious awareness is needed to improve. We must approach these in a self-regulatory manner, for example, with the use of on-going written reflection in the case of Reflective Goal Setting. This helps us to engage in self-monitoring by recording progress towards our goals.

Process- or performance-orientated—Which goals are best? Those focussed on performance such as getting a great grade in an exam, or process, such as developing more critical writing skills? Later in this book, we will look at the impact of process goals on academic growth and performance. But Reflective Goal Setting takes the approach that process goals are powerful when it comes to personal development. As one reflective goal setter explained:

> "When thinking back, I never really reflected on how well I achieved a goal or how I felt during the process. I only looked at the result, neglecting my happiness or well-being in the process."

Hierarchically organised—In an ideal situation, our goals are like Russian Dolls—nested hierarchically. This means that we may have one major distal goal, for example, getting a good degree grade, and smaller goals, for example, improving our reading around a topic. The smaller goals are the foundation of the achievement of the larger goal. Reflective Goal Setting generates proximal goals while keeping distal goals in mind.

WHY SHOULD WE WRITE ABOUT OUR GOALS?

> "Because I am writing it down, I am able to keep track of changes and respond to them. It also keeps reminding me that I am working towards a goal, which helps to motivate me."

A key fundamental feature of Reflective Goal Setting is writing about our goals—writing down the actual goals in detail and using on-going written reflection to assist the process. Previous research has shown that writing about and making sense of one's life experiences more generally, and pulling together otherwise fragmented stories and thoughts, has psychological and behavioural benefits (e.g., Lumley & Provenzano, 2003, Pennebaker, 1990). Myself, and a group of like-minded researchers have been trying to get to grips with why writing about goals is so powerful. On-going written reflection will be discussed in the next chapter, but for now let's look at the impact of writing our goals down.

In Canada, Morisano et al. (2010) carried out a study using an intensive, online, randomised controlled written goal setting intervention that required students to write about their ideal futures (personal life goals) for a total of about two and a half hours. They discovered increased academic achievement, improved retention rates, and a positive mood among academically struggling undergraduate students compared to those in the controlled condition. A key mediator was the total number of words written. An unexpected finding was that regardless of whether the students wrote about grade goals or other goals, academic results improved compared with the comparison group. Marschalka et al. in Romania (2018) replicated the study and found similar positive grade changes for struggling non-STEM students compared to a control group.

Building further on Morisano et al.'s work, Schippers et al. (2015) used a time-lagged quasi-experimental design comparing two cohorts of students with two pre-intervention cohorts. The intervention cohorts showed an increase in academic performance compared to the pre-intervention cohorts. Among the reasons for academic achievement were the number of words written, and quantity and quality of the plans they formulated regarding goal implementation. They too found that it didn't matter whether students wrote about academic goals, non-academic goals, or a combination of the two. Rather, it appeared to be the overall process of writing about their personal goals and degree of stage completion and effort that led to success (Schippers et al., 2015).

Reflective Goal Setting encourages a more extensive amount of writing and over a longer period of time than these other studies, but in many ways, the findings have been remarkably similar. We have all found that the process of writing about goals is likely to bring about greater motivation to take goal-directed action and more favourable goal outcomes than **not** writing about goals. Why might that be the case? Here are a few of the key reasons resulting from our collective work:

Writing about our goals in detail is better than creating 'to do lists'—Merely listing our goals seldom impacts outcomes. This is because the cognitive processing involved in listing is minimal and goal commitment, a moderator in goal setting theory, may not occur (Koestner et al., 2002). Writing out detailed strategies can mediate the goal setting–performance relationship. These plans can include recognition of potential obstacles and plans for overcoming them (Oettingen & Gollwitzer, 2010), which can increase self-efficacy. Furthermore, although there is a scarcity of research on the impact of personal goals, Emmons and Diener (1986) showed that simply having self-rated 'important' personal goals was as strongly correlated with positive affect as attaining them. Setting personal goals and making detailed plans may lead to an 'upward spiral' effect brought about by the self-reinforcing cycle of goal attainment (Sheldon & Houser-Marko, 2001), that cannot be achieved by writing constant wish lists. This upwards spiral effect is a key intention of Reflective Goal Setting.

Writing makes our goals concrete as opposed to abstract—Getting our goals 'out there' makes us more likely to achieve them (Höchli et al., 2018). Writing objectifies our goals and brings them into consciousness by means of the words chosen to outline them. They seem more real and so are more likely to be acted on. Writing can also make the goals seem public—which is more likely to lead to success (Epton et al., 2017). Reflective Goal Setting doesn't insist that goals are shared, but in many ways, the act of writing goals out on paper, or on our laptops, smart phones, or iPads, gets them 'out there'.

Writing enables on-going monitoring of our goals—Writing about our goals is an effective self-regulation strategy and any intervention that increases the frequency of monitoring is likely to promote behaviour change (Harkin et al., 2016). It is also easy to forget about our goals as we go about our day on autopilot. If we write about our goals, we bring them into conscious awareness, we direct our attention to them and continue to make them a priority, as writing creates a form of commitment. Reflective Goal Setting requires on-going written reflection on goal attempts and progress. Because the initial goal is written down in such detail, it is easier to compare on-going progress with this 'goal-blueprint'

A final word from a reflective goal setter:

> "I don't know what it is, or where it has come from, but I am starting to get this inner belief in me that I can do anything I set my mind to…for some strange reason I actually feel jubilant; so happy and content with myself…I absolutely love what it has done for me so far…this has enabled me to achieve things beyond what I thought I was capable of. …it has had a huge positive effect on my life."

SUMMARY

- Reflective Goal Setting builds on traditional Goal Setting Theory to enable the successful use of goal setting approaches for personal and soft skills development.
- The model utilises key features of goal-related theories but introduces the detailed writing out and the on-going reflective writing about goals.
- Writing about our goals is a powerful tool that leads to successful goal outcomes.
- There are many reasons for the impact of writing, but key is the writing of detailed plans, making goals concrete as opposed to abstract, and enabling the on-going monitoring of goals.

References

Aarts, H., & Custers, R. (2012). Unconscious goal pursuit: Nonconscious goal regulation and motivation. In R. M. Ryan (Ed.), *The Oxford handbook of human motivation* (pp. 232–247). Oxford University Press.

Bandura, A. (1986). *Social foundations of thought and action: A social cognitive theory*. Englewood Cliffs, NJ: Prentice-Hall.

Deci, E. L., & Ryan, R. M. (1985). The general causality orientations scale: Self-determination in personality. *Journal of Research in Personality, 19*(2), 109–134.

Doran, G. T. (1981). There's a S.M.A.R.T. way to write management's goals and objectives. Management Review, Volume 70, Issue 11(AMA FORUM), pp. 35–36.

Emmons, R. A., & Diener, E. (1986). Influence of impulsivity and sociability on subjective well-being. *Journal of Personality and Social Psychology, 50*(6), 1211–1215.

Epton, T., Currie, S., & Armitage, C. J. (2017). Unique effects of setting goals on behavior change: Systematic review and meta-analysis. *Journal of Consulting and Clinical Psychology, 85*(12), 1182.

Gollwitzer, P. M., & Sheeran, P. (2006). Implementation intentions and goal achievement: A meta-analysis of effects and processes. *Advances in Experimental Social Psychology, 38*, 69–119.

Haggis, T. (2002). Exploring the 'black box' of process: A comparison of theoretical notions of the 'adult learner' with accounts of postgraduate learning experience. *Studies in Higher Education, 27*(2), 207–220.

Harachi, T. W., Abbott, R. D., Catalano, R. F., Haggerty, K. P., & Fleming, C. B. (1999). Opening the black box: Using process evaluation measures to assess implementation and theory building. *American Journal of Community Psychology, 27*(5), 711–731.

Harkin, B., Webb, T. L., Chang, B. P., Prestwich, A., Conner, M., Kellar, I., Benn, Y., & Sheeran, P. (2016). Does monitoring goal progress promote goal attainment? A meta-analysis of the experimental evidence. *Psychological Bulletin, 142*(2), 198.

Höchli, B., Brügger, A., & Messner, C. (2018). How focusing on superordinate goals motivates broad, long-term goal pursuit: A theoretical perspective. *Frontiers in Psychology, 9*, 1879.

Koestner, R., Lekes, N., Powers, T. A., & Chicoine, E. (2002). Attaining personal goals: Self-concordance plus implementation intentions equals success. *Journal of Personality and Social Psychology, 83*(1), 231.

Latham, G. P., & Arshoff, A. S. (2015). Planning: A mediator in goal setting theory. In M. D. Mumford & M. Frese (Eds.), *The psychology of planning in organizations: Research and applications* (pp. 89–104). Routledge and Taylor & Francis Group.

Latham, G. P., & Locke, E. A. (1991). Self-regulation through goal setting. *Organizational Behavior and Human Decision Processes, 50*(2), 212–247.
Latham, G. P., & Locke, E. A. (2018). Goal setting theory: Controversies and resolutions. In D. S. Ones, N. Anderson, C. Viswesvaran, & H. K. Sinangil (Eds.), *The SAGE handbook of industrial, work & organizational psychology: Organizational psychology* (pp. 145–166). Sage Reference.
Locke, E. A. (1968). Toward a theory of task motivation and incentives. *Organizational Behavior and Human Performance, 3*(2), 157–189.
Locke, E. A., & Latham, G. P. (2002). Building a practically useful theory of goal setting and task motivation: A 35-year odyssey. *American Psychologist, 57*(9), 705.
Locke, E. A., & Latham, G. P. (Eds.). (2013). *New developments in goal setting and task performance.* Routledge and Taylor & Francis Group.
Lumley, M. A., & Provenzano, K. M. (2003). Stress management through written emotional disclosure improves academic performance among college students with physical symptoms. *Journal of Educational Psychology, 95*(3), 641.
Marschalko, E. E., Morisano, D., & Szamoskozi, I. (2018). Goal-setting among STEM and non-STEM students: A pilot randomised controlled trial. In E. Locke and M. Schippers (Eds), *Improving lives: Personal goal setting boosts student performance and happiness* (p. 1). Academy of Management Annual Meeting Proceedings. https://doi.org/10.5465/AMBPP.2018.16790symposium
Morisano, D., Hirsh, J. B., Peterson, J. B., Pihl, R. O., & Shore, B. M. (2010). Setting, elaborating, and reflecting on personal goals improves academic performance. *Journal of Applied Psychology, 95*(2), 255.
Oettingen, G., & Gollwitzer, P. (2010). *Strategies of setting and implementing goals: Mental contrasting and implementation intentions* (pp. 114–135). Guilford Press.
Pennebaker, J. W. (1990). *Opening up: The healing power of confiding in others.* William Morrow & Company.
Schippers, M. C., Scheepers, A. W., & Peterson, J. B. (2015). A scalable goal-setting intervention closes both the gender and ethnic minority achievement gap. *Palgrave Communications, 1*(1), 1–12.
Schunk, D. H. (1989). Social cognitive theory and self-regulated learning. In *Self-regulated learning and academic achievement* (pp. 83–110). Springer.
Sheldon, K. M., & Houser-Marko, L. (2001). Self-concordance, goal attainment, and the pursuit of happiness: Can there be an upward spiral? *Journal of Personality and Social Psychology, 80*(1), 152.
Sheldon, K. M., Kasser, T., Smith, K., & Share, T. (2002). Personal goals and psychological growth: Testing an intervention to enhance goal attainment and personality integration. *Journal of Personality, 70*(1), 5–31.
Zimmerman, B. J. (2008). Investigating self-regulation and motivation: Historical background, methodological developments, and future prospects. *American Educational Research Journal, 45*(1), 166–183.

CHAPTER 4

The Nature and Importance of Reflection and Keeping a Reflective Diary

What Can We Gain from Writing Reflectively About Our Goals?

Abstract This chapter will introduce you to a key underlying feature of Reflective Goal Setting—on-going written reflection. It will firstly outline what we mean by reflection and other associated terms such as reflexivity, whilst sharing some key theories and frameworks. Secondly, it will help you develop an appreciation for this important personal development and transfer of learning tool and equip you with the skills to write reflectively to support your Reflective Goal Setting activities.

Keywords Reflection • Reflexivity • On-going written reflective diary

INTRODUCTION

John "After a long day at lectures, got my act together and went to the gym. I went inside the changing rooms and there were no locks on the lockers. They are called lockers for a reason because they have

(continued)

© The Author(s), under exclusive license to Springer Nature Switzerland AG 2022
C. J. Travers, *Reflective Goal Setting*,
https://doi.org/10.1007/978-3-030-99228-6_4

a lock. That you lock! To keep your locker LOCKED!! I was angry, because I didn't get it, what is happening? I asked some guy and he said I needed to buy one for a couple of pounds. Well, isn't that just great? I pay hundreds to come here and need to pay extra for the locks. I was ready to go home and quit the gym right there and then. That was the most ridiculous thing I had ever seen.

Right?

Wrong!

I realized that that they do this so each person has a unique locker code which they can take home. This was a prime example of how I get stressed over little things, because they are not the way I would make them, when in fact, it isn't even important or relevant to why I was there. I should have been calm and ready to train and next time I will try to be more understanding. This isn't just a gym-related situation; it occurs often with me.

I went to the treadmill, which was really well-equipped with the newest tech to track progress. Unfortunately, there wasn't much to track, as I ran only 2.5 km barely. Disappointed, exhausted, and absolutely gutted that I couldn't run even 3 km. I went back to the dressing room to take a breath and get myself together. That was definitely the right choice to make. As with my previous experience earlier, this wasn't something to stress about. I knew there was a long way to go to run 10 km. I might not even be able to do this on 10th January as my goal had specified. But that's ok, I was there to develop my persistence in the face of challenges and things I don't like to do, and I was hyped to do it. Who would have thought—Me! Hyped about going to the gym! I was so proud I took my first steps, so I tried to stay positive and enjoy the moment, not worry about the future, because there was still a long road to go from here."

Jenny "Managed to get to the gym today. Didn't feel like it when I woke but my friend shamed me into doing it. Managed to do a set of circuits. Walked home past the kebab shop and undid a lot of my good work by having a huge kebab for my lunch. Felt guilty. Not good for my stress. Must try harder."

"Time and reflection change the sight little by little 'til we come to understand."—Paul Cezanne.

Above we have two examples of diary entries written by reflective goal setters, both of whom chose fitness-related goals to enhance their ability to manage stress in their final year of university. We will come back to them shortly. All five stages of Reflective Goal Setting (outlined next in Part 2) are underpinned by on-going written reflection. Reflective goal setters are invited to document their reflections from the onset of the process as they enhance their self-awareness, through goal ideation, visualisation, formulation, and implementation. There are many ways we can reflect, and though a select few have chosen to keep video diaries over the years, written reflective diaries are the preferred approach. The rationale for that will be discussed later, but for now let's define reflection, explore some key theories, and assess its effectiveness for personal development.

What Do We Mean by Reflection?

> "a highly personal, cognitive process… in which a person takes an experience from the outside world, brings it inside the mind, turns it over, makes connections to other experiences, and filters it through personal biases." (Dewey, 1910, p. 9)

The discussion of the impact of reflective thought in educational contexts mainly dates to the work of Dewey, with the term 'reflection' becoming more prominent in the discussion of personal and professional development in the 1980s with the work of Schön. Stemming from the Latin, 'reflectere' meaning 'to bend' or 'to turn back on the self,' reflection is not a modern concept. Plato advised that the philosophically 'good life' composed of wisdom, truth, and morality derived from this essential act.

Challenging to conceptualise (van Beveren et al., 2018), in its simplest form, reflection is 'thought' (van Manen, 1991) with definitions typically including some element of 'questioning' (Boud et al., 1985). It helps us explore, develop, and interact with others and the World about us (Boyd & Fales, 1983). Informed by our experiences, reflection is a deliberate cognitive activity, which frequently results in evaluation, criticality, and problem-solving to enhance our insight, awareness, and understanding. Much of our decision-making is 'impulsive' or 'routine' which may serve to reinforce and embed our current perceptions or practices—even when those prove to be ineffective or harmful for ourselves and/or others. For example, we may continue to engage in unhelpful responses to stress, or inappropriate ways of responding to criticism. The introduction of reflection can help mitigate this when used alongside the setting of goals.

Dewey's relatively scientific approach to reflection is not without criticism, with one issue being a lack of attention to the role of emotions (Salzberger-Wittenberg, 1983). However, his work was highly influential in the development of other models that followed—such as that of Schön (1983, 1987). Schön offers us a more intuitive and conscious view of reflection, encouraging us to draw on our experiences as the primary source of our learning:

> "The practitioner allows himself to experience surprise, puzzlement, or confusion in a situation which he finds uncertain or unique. He reflects on the phenomenon before him, and on the prior understandings which have been implicit in his behaviour. He carries out an experiment which serves to generate both a new understanding of the phenomenon and a change in the situation." (Schön, 1983, p. 68)

Schön further develops Dewey's notion of reflection with the concepts of *reflection-in-action* and *reflection-on-action*. Reflection-in-action takes place *during* an action, and reflection-on-action takes place *after* an event has occurred. Schön trained as a philosopher and a musician and implies that the 'body' and 'passion' of lived experience are part of reflective practice. His approach informs Reflective Goal Setting due to the nature of the types of skills it targets as 'lived' experiences, for example, listening more effectively, managing emotional reactions to stressful events, presenting more charismatically, etc.

Schön encourages us to see each experience as unique, but to draw on what has gone before. He doesn't fully clarify what is involved in the reflective process, and it may be challenging to stop and make the time to engage in 'reflection in action.' This is where '*reflection on action*' may come in. The act of reflecting *following* an event or action enables us to spend time, somewhere away from the busy throng, or line of fire, exploring why we acted as we did, what was happening in our team, and so on. The following example from a university undergraduate reflective goal setter involved in job search activities shows how written reflection— 'reflection *on* action'—can develop subsequent 'reflection *in* action.'

> "The first example of goal achievement was on the 3rd of November where I was able to turn a graduate training scheme rejection into an opportunity for learning. In the past, having a rejection would have caused self-doubt, upset or loss of motivation; however, by documenting the experience in my diary, I reflected and felt accountable for my behaviour, could see what I might need to do differently, and was able to overcome negativity and feeling of not being in control. Furthermore, on the 7th of December—due to these earlier reflective insights—I was able to positively tackle another rejection email as it arrived. I was instantly able to focus on the positives as I was reading it, such as my unsuitability for the role, benefits of the experience, as well as gratitude—mitigating past critical behaviour."

A related concept, developed from Schön's work, is *reflection*-**for**-*action* (Killion & Todnem, 1991). This is when we think about *future* actions with the intention of improving or changing a practice. Reflective Goal Setting makes good use of all three aspects. Via its five stages and on-going written reflection, the model seeks to develop and utilise *reflection* **on** *action* through the mechanisms of written reflection, *reflection* **in** *action* when actual goal attempts take place, and *reflection* **for** *action* with the generation of ideas for how to perform effective goal behaviours in the future. For example:

> "I generally am blinded by how far I have got to go and forget how far I have come. Using a reflective diary encouraged me to look back at my efforts to see if these were really working. In times of success, I was able to build on behaviours to take the next step in reaching my goal. When I had come to a hurdle, I could re-evaluate my efforts and take a different path if required."

The written reflective diary will be discussed later in the chapter.

WHY SHOULD WE USE REFLECTION FOR PERSONAL AND LEADER DEVELOPMENT?

Traditionally, reflection tends to feature in the education of those professions seen as 'helping,' such as nursing (McAndrew & Roberts, 2015), midwifery, (Wain, 2017) and teaching (Pollard, 2002). Frequently referred to as '*Reflective Practice*,' it provides opportunities to explore how roles are carried out 'in practice' using reflective approaches (Karm, 2010). The capacity to reflect relates directly to how effectively individuals can learn from their personal experiences and therefore provides a meaningful addition to any approach aimed at enhancing personal development. The main objective for integrating reflection in leadership development programmes is to maximize leader potential by allowing participants to evaluate the significance of their experiences from a leadership perspective. A key rationale for the development of Reflective Goal Setting was my observation that leaders and managers were increasingly required to be instrumental in the development and wellbeing of their employees and teams, as well as their own. However, research suggests that leader self-awareness is lacking and the results from leader personal development activities are disappointing in many contexts. This, for me, justifies the use of reflective approaches in the education of managers, leaders, and would-be leaders.

Reflective practice is often considered the "favoured paradigm for professional development" (Clegg et al., 2002, p. 131), despite not being seen as desirable by all (Fanghanel, 2012). There are difficulties with teaching people how to reflect (Smith, 2011) and reflective practice has been associated with a 'dark side' that "can result in people being seduced by their own stories and beliefs" (Hickson, 2011, p. 832). The use of an on-going written reflective diary is a powerful way of developing the skill, increasing sense-making, and reducing the potential for self-deceit. For example:

> "I was very surprised when I noticed that I initially reacted negatively to a situation but then stepped away from that room and came back more positively. It proved that reflection actually was affecting my decision-making, which I think I will carry with me for the rest of my life."

Critical reflection can be uncomfortable, potentially creating dissonance in the reflector (Brookfield, 1995). However, the alternative may be consistently poor decision-making and bad judgment. For example, in the quest to achieve a vision, a leader may be so driven by personal ambition that they ignore or fail to question the consequences of their actions. Without reflection, leaders may be convinced that their past successes make them invincible and fail to consider other viewpoints, with possibly disastrous consequences. Similarly, leaders may avoid reflecting on a course of action because such reflection might challenge their favourable perceptions of themselves (Conger, 1990).

When we become truly and effectively reflective, we embody a skill and are then able to model it for others. An embodied approach allows a sense of order to be brought to our descriptions of our experiences, which are then brought into our conscious awareness (Leigh & Bailey, 2013). But, new ways of thinking and behaving do not necessarily result just from having an experience and then thinking about it (Miles, 2011). Indeed, Weiss cautions us that, "mental reflection is a very dubious process, always prone to bend and distort towards social desirability, defence of our behaviour, and habitual thought patterns" (Weiss, 2009, p. 9). Hence, Reflective Goal Setting uses an on-going written reflective diary as a place for 'workings out' of thoughts, feelings, and ideas about what, why, and how we can take things forward. Writing can help us make sense of our experiences and challenge any assumptions we may have developed—especially when reflection is combined with well-formulated goals. This approach likely develops *reflexivity* as opposed to just reflection (Hatton & Smith, 1995). Reflexivity is when we focus our close attention on our actions, thoughts, feelings, values, identity, and their effect upon others, situations, and professional and social structures. The in-depth self-awareness activity carried out at Stage 1 of the model, outlined later in Chap. 5, supports the development of this reflexive approach.

How Can We Develop the Ability to be Reflective?

If we want to develop reflection to aid our learning, we can look to various theoretical frameworks and models for guidance. Probably the most well-known is Kolb's (1984) four stage experiential learning cycle, fusing goal-directed and behavioural learning theories to create four distinct learning styles: **Concrete Experience**: Where we encounter a new situation or experience; or reinterpret an existing one. **Reflective Observation of the New Experience:** Where we examine any inconsistencies between this experience and our current understanding. **Abstract Conceptualization**: Where our reflection brings up a new idea or alters an existing abstract concept (so we have learned from our experience). **Active Experimentation**: We apply our new idea to the world around us and see what results from our chosen action. Honey and Mumford (1989) devised four learning styles based loosely around Kolb's four stages: Activists, Reflectors, Theorists, and Pragmatists which have proved popular in training and development settings. However, criticisms have levelled that clear-cut learning stages do not equate to most people's reality, that the models lack methodological rigour and empirical support, and that insufficient emphasis is placed on the power of reflection on learning (e.g., Tennant, 1997; Boud et al., 1985).

One model that I have successfully shared with my students is the six-stage Reflective Cycle of Gibbs (1988)—a model widely used for educational purposes. The stages are:

1. Describing what happened,
2. An examination of feelings and thoughts related to this,
3. Evaluation of the positive and negative aspects,
4. Subsequent analysis where sense is made,
5. Conclusions drawn regarding what else can be done,
6. Action planning for involving actions that may be applied within future re-occurrence.

Though I have always encouraged free writing in reflective diaries, these six stages can support written reflections and reflective goal setters talk fondly of Gibbs' cycle and the role it plays in their goal setting.

> Take another look at the two examples of diary entries at the start of this chapter and see if you can identity Gibb's cycle.
>
> - Which one do you see as the most reflective and why? (Hopefully you chose John's!)
> - Take another look at Jenny's diary, what else might she have written to make that a truly reflective diary entry?
> - Which one is most like the kind of diary entry **you** would typically write?

Alongside these models and frameworks, there are several personal attributes that Dewey (1933) suggested are needed: **open-mindedness**—where we consider more alternative sides of an issue and recognise the importance of questioning our firmest beliefs; **responsibility**—where we actively search for truth and apply any information gained to problem situations; **wholeheartedness**—where we can overcome fears and uncertainties to enable meaningful change and self-evaluation, and critique of our organizations, and society. A lack of involvement in our own learning might restrict the use/development of these attributes (Main, 1985). Stage 1 of Reflective Goal Setting begins with a critical analysis of our experiences via observations to develop the motivation and skill to engage in goal-related reflection-in-action. Experience is more than just an event and involves our perceptions of those events, and how we actively shape and construct our experiences by selectively attending to certain situations. Our views are affected by feelings, needs, prior experiences, and expectations (Hughes et al., 1999). Often, we are unaware of our perceptual biases. So, Reflective Goal Setting helps provide opportunities for the enhanced understanding of our perception and interpretation of observations of our own behaviour.

THE ROLE OF WRITING REFLECTIVELY IN REFLECTIVE GOAL SETTING

In Reflective Goal Setting, we are encouraging a variety of ways of reflecting, but mainly through the use of an on-going written reflective diary. The suggestion is that we begin to write reflectively from the start of the process, documenting our discoveries about our self-awareness, our ideas for goals, what we are aiming for, the formation of our goals, and then each time we make a goal attempt.

What Do We Mean by a Reflective Diary?

Traditionally, we consider a diary to be a frequently kept—often daily—record of personal experiences and observations in which on-going thoughts, feelings and ideas can be expressed. Diaries can help us monitor changes over time (e.g., Travers, 2011; Daniels & Harris, 2005). Hence, they are useful when combined with on-going goal setting for personal development. So, in our context, reflective diary keeping benefits the goal setter whilst also enabling us to gain insights into how Reflective Goal Setting works.

Some scholars and practitioners distinguish between the various written forms of diaries, logs, and journals. Diaries are personal, unstructured, and usually private. Logs are records of information that are highly structured, with factual accounts, maintained over time. Journals combine the objective aspects of the log with the personal aspect of a diary and tend to take on a more reflective learning slant. The contemporary focus on learning and reflection in diaries or journals shifts the emphasis to process rather than product and makes them a helpful tool within educational environments. (e.g., Loo & Thorpe, 2002). Journaling can also help develop observational skills—in our case, of our own behaviour (Callister, 1993). Redfern (1995) further argues that writing helps us transfer our thoughts onto paper for examination and analysis in a less personal, more objective way. The process of constructing words and sentences in one's head before committing these to paper enables thoughts and recollections of events to be given a certain degree of structure and accuracy. The diary also acts as a permanent record of our goal attempts which can be used to gain further insights later. We use 'diary' to combine elements of both journals and logs, as both aspects can be of use throughout the Reflective Goal Setting process depending on goals chosen and approaches taken.

How Frequently Should We Keep a Reflective Diary and How Much Should We Write

> "I think keeping the diary so regularly allowed me to maintain an active interest in accomplishing my goal. Knowing that I would have to put down in words where I had failed my goal made me much more committed to it. Knowing that I would be held externally accountable helped too."

Reflective goal setters are not required to keep daily diaries, but one retrospective reflective entry on a Sunday evening following a week of goal setting might limit the benefits. Recording efforts, emotions, thoughts, and feelings about goal attempts works best when undertaken as close to a goal attempt as possible. Timely written diaries reduce the likelihood of retrospection as the minimum amount of time elapses between an experience and its recall. This is important for recall accuracy, as Bartlett (1932) noted, "Remembering is… the past being continually remade, reconstructed in the interest of the present." When it comes to writing about our goal attempts, it is crucial that we write accurately and honestly. Diary writing also requires some commitment to routine and self-discipline—much like hygiene rituals such as cleaning teeth.

In practice, reflective goal setters have tended to keep diaries ranging from every day to two or three times per week while working on their goals. The amount written in not prescribed in the model, and actual numbers of words written varies from goal setter to goal setter. Some produce the equivalent of around half a side of A4 per diary entry, others write for pages and pages. The *reflective quality* of the writing is perhaps the most important aspect. Some use the diary to document many other peripheral activities as well as their goal attempts—hence creating much longer diaries. But the power seems to be in working through the types of reflective process as set out by Gibbs, and a couple of written lines are not going to achieve that. Future work is planned to examine the impact of amount of writing, frequency and types of words used on goal success. But for now it is suffice to say that, regularity, timeliness, and reflective depth appear to be powerful aids to goal setting. It is helpful to think of the diary as an accurate and detailed record of your goal setting as it is 'lived.' Whilst writing, you get a sense of how you are progressing and can look back on any past entries which documented successful attempts—especially helpful when goal motivation or achievement is low. Writing can motivate us to keep pushing forward and 'getting back on the goal-horse.' Reflective goal setters talk about how committed they feel to keep going. For example:

> "Reflective Goal Setting is like being part of a committed relationship, you have to stay on top of putting time into the relationship—even in the long-term. I chose this metaphor as I believe it is easy to skip reflection and neglect writing experiences down, but it pays off if you can stay on top of it. Just like consistent energy into a committed relationship."

What Form Should the Diaries Take?

In the early days of Reflective Goal Setting, I encouraged handwritten reflections and diaries. Handwriting can be a mechanism for self-discovery and sense-making. Pennebaker and Segal (1999) have suggested that disclosure through writing may be best understood as promoting the creation of narrative sources of meaning and that writing is a way of making sense of one's life experience and pulling together otherwise fragmented stories, memoirs, and experiences. Due to changes in the use of word processing and related technologies, goal setters have been given the choice to handwrite or word-process—with many more choosing the word-processing option with no obvious detrimental effect on the quality or power of their reflections. Contemporary goal setters are used to working online, note taking on their phones and computers, and are more comfortable doing so. Both options have their advantages and disadvantages.

When choosing to write by hand, many goal setters report taking time to find a suitable notebook and pen, personalising them, and sticking relevant things in, such as photos. A physical diary provides something tangible, and the feel of paper in our hands can be gratifying. It is easily transportable, though we must be careful not to leave it on the train or allow it to fall into the wrong hands. It is also our only copy, but we don't have to worry about getting hacked! Writing by hand also prevents us going back through and changing our reflections, because we want it to be an authentic piece of writing.

James and Engelhardt (2012) found that typing on a keyboard and writing by hand are all associated with distinct and separate brain patterns. When children compose text by hand, they not only consistently produce more words and more quickly than they do on a keyboard, but they express more ideas. Writing by hand requires more subtle and complicated motion from your fingers than typing, it increases activity in the brain's motor cortex, an effect like meditation. This explains why journaling can feel therapeutic and why it helps with mindfulness. On the other hand, the potential inconvenience of handwriting can lead to messy scribbles that are hard to read and we may run out of steam or feel hampered by the presentation of our handwriting.

If we choose to word process, for example, via Microsoft Word, OneNote, WordPress, etc, the keyboard can be used to draw thoughts out of our head and onto the screen. This might be more convenient, and the end-product is much the same as writing long-hand. Some may find it easier to type, especially as many of us are used to spending much of our day in front of a screen and are faster at typing than writing. Creativity isn't exclusively the result of writing by hand. Plenty of great writers type their manuscripts. There may well be more distractions when we work on a computer, but we can find ways of blocking out distractions. In fact, we may be able to adhere to the habit of writing and generate more words if we type diaries. Some may well type faster and engage with a stream of consciousness. It might be possible to type through emotions and visualise thoughts on screen. When you type, you can create backups of your diary and, using the right tools, you can access your diary from anywhere. Plus, it's easier to search for specific entries and words used, for example, how many times you use positive language as you progress.

Overall, it's a personal choice and whichever is chosen, the diary is a powerful tool as this reflective goal setter explains:

> "I didn't realize the power of keeping a diary, this has allowed me to have a lot less mental chatter and be more relaxed, not dwelling on situations that occur."

What Skills Do We Need to Write a Reflective Diary?

There is no requirement to be a literary genius in order to write a reflective diary. It doesn't have to be beautifully written with perfect grammar and spelling. These diaries are not intended for an eventual audience, like those of Samuel Pepys or Anne Frank. Many diarists take a while to get into their reflective flow and some need prompts, like those provided by Gibbs suggested earlier. Others prefer to write freely and are natural writers, though they can often stray from the main purpose—to write about our goals as they unfold. It is more about having a particular mindset and a willingness to critically reflect which, Reynolds (1999, p. 538) advises, involves "a commitment to questioning assumptions and taken-for-granteds embodied in both theory and professional practice." Authenticity and enthusiasm also go a long way.

Which type of reflective goal setting diary will you go for? If you are still in doubt as to how helpful one can be, a final word from a senior manager working in the automotive industry who employed Reflective Goal Setting:

> "Moving to a new site, with a new team, full of strong and experienced characters I found myself trying to find different ways to engage these six very different characters. I revisited my notes on Reflective Goal Setting and started to keep another diary recording my interactions and coaching moments with team members and using my notes to form a specific goal and approach before engaging in any further meetings. I would note the conversation and my personal thoughts on the outcome. From this, I developed a tailored approach to each individual and the on-going reflection allowed me to quickly recall previous conversations when coaching moments arose.
>
> During the first 3 months of my taking this approach, overall engagement has increased, with members showing greater enthusiasm when trying new processes or adapting current ones. The sales rate from 3 individuals has considerably increased—one member who previously only sold 6 vehicles in 5 weeks, now selling 37 in an 8-week period!"

Summary

- Reflection is a powerful tool for supporting the transfer of our learning, especially related to soft skills.
- There are several models we can use to guide our reflections.
- It is a worthy contributor to the design of personal development and leader programmes.
- Written reflection is especially powerful, but writing should be done close to the event, in our case, goal attempts.
- Handwritten or word processed diaries can work equally well.

References

Bartlett, F. C. (1932). *Remembering: A study in experimental and social psychology.* Cambridge University Press.

Boud, D., Keogh, R., & Walker, D. (1985). *Reflection: Turning experience into learning.* Routledge.

Boyd, E. M., & Fales, A. W. (1983). Reflective learning: Key to learning from experience. *Journal of Humanistic Psychology, 23*(2), 99–117.

Brookfield, S. (1995). *Becoming a critically reflective teacher.* Jossey-Bass.

Callister, L. C. (1993). The use of student journals in nursing education: Making meaning out of clinical experience. *Journal of Nursing Education, 32*(4), 185–186.

Clegg, S., Tan, J., & Saedidi, S. (2002). Reflecting or acting? Reflective practice and continuing professional development in Higher Education. *Reflective Practice, 3*, 131–146.

Conger, J. A. (1990). The dark side of leadership. *Organizational Dynamics, 19*(2), 44–55.

Daniels, K., & Harris, C. (2005). A daily diary study of coping in the context of the job demands–control–support model. *Journal of Vocational Behavior, 66*(2), 219–237.

Dewey, J. (1910). Science as subject-matter and as method. *Science, 31*(787), 121–127.

Dewey, J. (1933). *How we think.* Heath.

Fanghanel, J. (2012). *Being an academic.* Routledge.

Gibbs, G. (1988). *Learning by doing: A guide to teaching and learning methods.* Further Education Unit. Oxford Polytechnic.

Hatton, N., & Smith, D. (1995). Reflection in teacher education: Towards definition and implementation. *Teaching and Teacher Education, 11*, 33–49.

Hickson, H. (2011). Critical reflection: Reflecting on learning to be reflective. *Reflective Practice: International and Multidisciplinary Perspectives, 12*, 829–839.

Honey, P., & Mumford, A. (1989). *Learning styles questionnaire.* Organization Design and Development, Incorporated.

Hughes, R. L., Ginnett, R. C., & Curphy, G. J. (1999). *Leadership: Enhancing the lessons of experiences.* McGraw-Hill.

James, K. H., & Engelhardt, L. (2012). The effects of handwriting experience on functional brain development in pre-literate children. *Trends in Neuroscience and Education, 1*(1), 32–42.

Karm, M. (2010). Reflection tasks in pedagogical training courses. *International Journal for Academic Development, 15*(3), 203–214.

Killion, J. P., & Todnem, G. R. (1991). A process for personal theory building. *Educational Leadership, 48*(6), 14–16.

Kolb, D. A. (1984). *Experiential learning: Experiences as a source of learning and development.* Prentice-Hall.

Leigh, J., & Bailey, R. (2013). Reflection, reflective practice and embodied reflective practice. *Body, Movement and Dance in Psychotherapy, 8,* 160–171.

Loo, R., & Thorpe, K. (2002). Using reflective learning journals to improve individual and team performance. *Team Performance Management: An International Journal, 8,* 134–139.

Main, A. (1985). Reflection and the development of learning skills. In *Reflection: Turning experience into learning* (pp. 91–99). Kogan Page.

McAndrew, S., & Roberts, D. (2015). Reflection in nurse education: Promoting deeper thinking through the use of painting. *Reflective Practice, 16*(2), 206–217.

Miles, A. (2011). The reflective coach. In I. Stafford (Ed.), *Coaching children in sport* (pp. 109–120). Routledge.

Pennebaker, J.W. and Segal, J.D. (1999). Forming a survey: The health benefits of narrative. *Journal of Clinical Psychology, 55,* 1243–1254.

Pollard, A. (2002). *Readings for reflective teaching.* A&C Black.

Redfern, E. (1995). Profiles, portfolios and reflective practice: Part 2. *Professional Update, 3,* 10.

Reynolds, M. (1999). 'Grasping the nettle: possibilities and pitfalls of a critical management pedagogy', *British Journal of Management 10*(2), 171–184.

Salzberger-Wittenberg, I. (1983). Part 1: Beginnings. In I. Salzberger-Wittenberg, G. Henry, & E. Osborne (Eds.), *The emotional experience of teaching and learning.* Routledge and Kegan Paul.

Schön, D. A. (1983). *The reflective practitioner: How professionals think in action.* Basic Books. (Reprinted in 1995).

Schön, D. A. (1987). *Educating the reflective practitioner.* Jossey-Bass.

Smith, E. (2011). Teaching critical reflection. *Teaching in Higher Education, 16,* 211–223.

Tennant, M. (1997). *Psychology and adult learning* (2nd ed.). Routledge.

Travers, C. (2011). Unveiling a reflective diary methodology for exploring the lived experiences of stress and coping. *Journal of Vocational Behavior*, *79*(1), 204–216.

Van Beveren, L., Roets, G., Buysse, A., & Rutten, K. (2018). We all reflect, but why? A systematic review of the purposes of reflection in higher education in social and behavioral sciences. *Educational Research Review*, *24*, 1–9.

Van Manen, M. (1991). Reflectivity and the pedagogical moment: The normativity of pedagogical thinking and acting. *Journal of Curriculum Studies*, *23*(6), 507–536.

Wain, A. (2017). Examining the lived experiences of newly qualified midwives during their preceptorship. *British Journal of Midwifery*, *25*(7), 451–457.

Weiss, H. (2009). The use of mindfulness in psychodynamic and body orientated psychotherapy. *Body, Movement and Dance in Psychotherapy*, *4*, 5–16.

PART II

The Reflective Goal Setting Model

CHAPTER 5

Stage 1: Enhancing Self-Awareness

What Should We Discover About Ourselves in Order to Set Personal and Leader Development Goals?

Abstract This first chapter of Part II outlines the key features of Stage 1 and shares a selection of helpful concepts, frameworks, and tools for gaining greater self-insight. Opportunities will be provided for you to have a go at some for yourself. An understanding of how to use this stage to good effect will be gained, providing the basis for Stage 2 and the rest of the model.

Keywords Self-awareness · Self-insight · Life story · Development needs · Authenticity · Feedback

Introduction

Don't mock the importance of self-awareness!
Anyone who has ever watched the TV mockumentary sitcom 'The Office' (UK or US version) will be aware of the fictional character—in the US, Michael Scott (played by Steve Carell) and in the UK, David Brent (played by Ricky Gervais). This fictitious regional manager of a fictitious paper distribution company in a non-descript town is the central character of the series and someone who demonstrably has no self-awareness whatsoever. He has a largely innocent disposition, but frequently exhibits a destructive persona, though he perceives himself as having lofty ideals and great leadership skills. He talks of his workforce as if they are his 'family.' And he spouts great managerial wisdom to the cameras which follow him and his employees around day to day.

He gets into many scrapes due to his lack of insight, self-awareness, know-how, and insensitivity when dealing with anyone who is not white, male, and heterosexual. His character especially lacks an understanding of boundaries, and he causes frequent problems for his staff due to his inability to keep his mouth firmly shut about their secrets and private lives. Usually politically incorrect and inappropriate, one classic line from Michael is when he introduces his receptionist, Pam, to a new member of staff and says: "This is our receptionist Pam, and if you think she's cute now, you should've seen her a couple of years ago!"

Many people might recognise glimpses of someone they know in this character—a colleague or manager, though it is hard to believe that in this supposedly enlightened age we may still witness these kinds of behaviours. There are so many courses, policies, and programmes attempting to develop managers' and leaders' emotional intelligence and self-insight. However, watching 'The Office' does make me squirm as I have witnessed several instances of similar characters and behaviour in my many years as an educator, consultant, and trainer. Luckily not too many. But as the popular quote advises, we usually leave managers, not jobs or organisations. Let's take an example of some 'office-esque' manager behaviour:

Many years ago, a manager arrived as a delegate on a course I was delivering on basic management skills. He had been managing for some

(continued)

years, and so it seemed rather odd at first. His senior manager had signed him up for the programme, though in his mind he had 'volunteered.' The prompt—or we might say final straw—had been his approach to interviewing candidates for a forklift truck driver post. A female member of staff had applied, and he enquired of her in the interview "What would a nice pretty, young girl like you be doing applying for a job so physical like this when you might have to lift heavy things? It's not for you, my love! What do you think?" She'd smiled sweetly and promptly headed to HR to complain on her way from the interview.

Michael Scott lives!

These illustrations might seem extreme, and they are, but even those managers and leaders with the best intentions can lack self-insight and authenticity.

"Ninety per cent of the world's woes come from people not knowing themselves, their abilities, their frailties, and even their real virtues. Most of us go almost all the way through life as complete strangers to ourselves."—Sidney Harris

As we saw in Chap. 1, my interest in self-awareness goes back many years, but the term has recently become a 'buzzword' due to the perception of its contemporary importance (Ardelt & Grunwald, 2018), especially when it comes to leaders (Steffens et al., 2021). However, it is not a recent concept. Knowing oneself and introspection are as old as ancient Greece and may well have played a key part in the rise of human civilization (Leary & Buttermore, 2003). Philosophers, theologians, psychologists, and social commentators have long emphasized the critical importance of accurate self-knowledge for attaining success and fulfilment. Definitions vary, but in a nutshell, self-awareness refers to an inwardly focused, evaluative process in which we compare ourselves to others and salient standards (e.g., a behaviour or progress towards a goal) with the aim of better self-knowledge and improvement (Ashley & Reiter-Palmon, 2012; Duval & Wicklund, 1972).

> **Moment for Reflection: Me, Myself, and I**
> Ask yourself the following questions:
>
> Which three words best sum up the essence of who I am?
> What do I feel I contribute when at work?
> What do I want others to value me for?
> What do I think is the biggest misconception people have of me?

In the early 1900s, Charles Cooley talked of the *'looking-glass self'* to describe how a person grows and matures out of society's interpersonal interactions and the perceptions others have of them (Cooley, 1902), also referred to by Steven Covey as 'Social Mirror Theory' (2013). Covey however offers a note of caution: "If the only vision we have of ourselves comes from the social mirror—from the current social paradigm and the opinions, perceptions and paradigms of the people around us—our view of ourselves is like the reflection in the crazy mirror room at the carnival."

Reflective Goal Setting will show you how to gain an all-round, self-generated view of self, using other more effective and accurate forms of reflection than those coming from a fairground mirror.

> **Moment for Reflection**
> Think about all the people you deal with.
> What gets reflected back at you regarding how they see you?
> Are their views consistent or varied?
> Why might that be the case?
> How accurate do you honestly think those views are?

As an organizational psychologist working in this field for many years, I have seen how attainable and powerful enhanced self-awareness can be, yet it is in relatively short supply. Eurich (2018) claims that self-awareness is a rare quality—estimating that only 10%–15% of people fit the criteria. This is especially the case in the workplace, where researchers suggest we are even less self-aware (Dierdorff & Rubin, 2015). The means to develop it, motivation to gain it, and tactics to sustain it are lacking along with a failure to match it with desirable performance and outcomes. Hence, the importance of the first key stage of Reflective Goal Setting.

There are many benefits to be gleaned from gaining self-awareness—especially in organizational settings. Evidence suggests: more effective decision-making (Scott Ridley et al., 1992); stronger relationships (Fletcher & Bailey, 2003); more effective communication (Sutton et al., 2015); better managerial performance (Church, 1997); greater chance of promotion and leader effectiveness (Bass & Yammarino, 1991), among others.

There can also be downsides to extensive introspection, however. Whilst engaging in self-reflection, we will typically find shortcomings in ourselves. For example, if we want to be a more successful leader, our focus of attention will be discrepancies between how we lead, and our leader aspirations. Similarly, if we are unfit and neglecting our health, reflection on our exercise habits will likely highlight that our physical activity falls short of the ideal. Attention focused on 'intraself discrepancy' might result in *proportional* negative affect, demotivation, and a lack of positive outcomes. This explains why self-awareness activity has often received bad press in fields such as social-clinical psychology because of its potential ties to such responses as negative affect and depression (Silvia & O'Brien, 2004). Research suggests that the positive and negative facets of self-awareness are reconciled when people have reasonable self-standards and when they are optimistic about meeting those standards. Reflective Goal Setting helps us gain self-awareness by drawing on a range of sources—to explore our strengths and development needs—accompanied by goal setting, role models, and visualisation of future behaviours to lead to a more constructive and realistic self-evaluation.

When seeking to gain greater self-awareness, a few key psychological concepts are worthy of our attention. Firstly, the *self-concept* which can be defined as a complex, organised, and dynamic framework of learned beliefs, attitudes, and opinions that we each of us holds to be true about our personal existence. Self-concept differs from *self-esteem* (our feelings of personal worth and level of satisfaction regarding oneself), *self-efficacy* (perception of competence in a particular domain), or *self-report* (what we are willing and able to disclose). Many of our experienced successes and failures are closely related to how we have learnt to view ourselves and our relationships with others. How we approach goals and the confidence and belief we have in our ability to succeed at them links to our self-efficacy (e.g., Bandura, 1977). Gaining self-awareness can help us develop a more stable self-concept—one that is more consistent and less affected by events.

Secondly, Social Comparison Theory asserts that we learn about our personal attitudes through engaging in a process of comparison with others (Festinger, 1957). Upward social comparison is where we compare ourselves to someone who we feel is better than us. As opposed to downward social comparison—comparing to someone who we see as worse. Both can be destructive and not helpful when seeking a realistic sense of self. Enhanced self-awareness can help us develop a more realistic view so that we can set relevant and appropriate goals. With social media as it is, the opportunity and frequency of opportunities—helpful and less helpful—for comparison are bordering on the infinite. For example, one Reflective Goal Setter reported:

> "I want a piece of the success that everyone around me seems to achieve. All I have to do is go on Instagram to realise how little I am achieving at the moment and be reminded of all the amazing things other people are doing. In fact, it's not even just Instagram—Strava, everyone on Strava posts these amazing runs they have done, or 90 km bike rides on their Sunday which they achieve before I have even got out of bed. I wish this was me."

Without enhanced self-awareness, we may not realise the potentially unrealistic and damaging impact of social comparison on how we see ourselves, be able to grasp the perspectives others may have on our behaviour, exercise self-control, produce creative accomplishments, or experience pride and high self-esteem.

According to Eurich (2018), we have two types of self-awareness. The clarity with which we know about ourselves, for example, our feelings, thoughts, and values and how they impact on others is our *internal* self-awareness. This is linked to higher job and relationship satisfaction, personal and social control, and happiness; and negatively related to anxiety, stress, and depression. External self-awareness, on the other hand, is our understanding of how other people view us. This is linked to the skills of empathy and taking others' perspectives. Reflective Goal Setting aims to enhance both.

The Johari Window (Luft & Ingham, 1955) provides a useful matrix of self and others' knowledge of us. It is a framework for understanding conscious and unconscious bias that can help increase our self-awareness and understanding of others. Combinations give us the Open Self, The Hidden Self, the Unknown Self, and the Blind self (see Fig. 5.1).

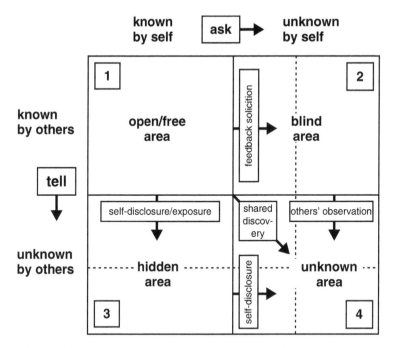

Fig. 5.1 Johari window. Based on Luft & Ingham (1955) and Luft (1961)

I encourage my goal setters to work on reducing the size of the 'blind-self' and 'unknown' panes. Stage 1 supports personal disclosure and feedback to increase the size of the 'open' arena.

So, let's look at the key features of Stage 1 and how to use it.

Firstly, Identify and Engage with Relevant Self-Awareness Activities

If you have ever participated in a training or development programme, chances are you engaged in some form of self-assessment designed to increase self-awareness. Self-awareness activities might include things like the Myers Briggs Type Indicator (MBTI), (Myers, 1962), as well as other more specific measures of traits and attitudes. While you may have discovered your 'type,' 'profile,' or 'style,' there is no guarantee that greater personal effectiveness was the outcome. As I outlined in Chap. 2, this may be due to poor transfer of learning—possibly due to a lack of proper goal setting.

Many self-report assessments target self-knowledge, but as the Dunning-Kruger effect suggests, we can be notoriously poor judges of our own capabilities and are more likely to overestimate our knowledge or competence compared to others, especially when we are less skilled (Kruger & Dunning, 1999).

> **Moment for Reflection**
> Have you ever had reason to be surprised at your lack of self-knowledge?

We may eagerly lap up the results of self-knowledge assessments and presume they are accurate, but without other external data, results may reinforce and perpetuate inaccurate self-perceptions. The net result may be harmful to our performance and development. So, it is important to harvest a variety of sources, triangulate these, and look for key themes and patterns.

> **Have a Go at a Self-Awareness Activity: The Twenty Statements Test**
> Kuhn and McPartland (1954) devised the Twenty Statements Test. This is based on a sociological theory called Symbolic Interactionism (Mead, 1934). It is not without its critics (e.g., Watkins et al., 1997), but when combined with other approaches, my goal setters have found it invaluable over the years. For example:
> "The Twenty Statements Test brought a realisation that I had several negative connotations of how I would describe myself as a person. It took a great deal of thought to conjure 20 things that accurately describe me. I consider myself a happy and positive person evident in early positive words such as "happy" and "sociable", but towards the end I wrote words including "lazy" and "average". This fostered a realisation that there are areas of myself that require development, to rid these connotations from my own description in order to improve my self-esteem."
> So, have a go:
> There are 20 numbered blanks below. Please write 20 different answers to the question 'Who am I?' in the blanks. Write the answers in the order they occur to you. Don't worry about logic or importance.

(continued)

Who am I?
1.
2.
3.
4.
5.
6.
7.
8.
9.
10.
11.
12.
13.
14.
15.
16.
17.
18.
19.
20.

Moment for Reflection
Overall, how positive, or self-critical, is your list?
What is your list telling you about how you see yourself?
How many of the things chosen were 'gifted' to you by others?
How do they affect how you view yourself?
How accurate are they?
What might your list suggest about ideas for personal development?

Next, Gather and Evaluate Feedback

It is helpful to become aware of how (in)consistently our self-view compares to external appraisal by others, or against objective data (i.e., accuracy of our work, academic performance etc.). With the rising popularity of feedback for performance improvement in all walks of life and especially work organisations, such as multi-rater or 360-degree feedback (e.g., Church, 1995; Hazucha et al., 1993; London & Beatty, 1993), many of us have been exposed to a variety of feedback.

In order to personally develop and grow, we need a clear idea of what we're doing well, what can be improved upon, and how our actions are being perceived. Asking for feedback is good, though others may be hesitant to give feedback with honesty and objectivity. So, how you approach it is critical for truthful dialogue. As part of Stage 1, you could: Ask others for feedback; make it clear that you are ready to receive, reflect, and respond to the feedback given; ask for specific feedback on areas that you have identified as important for development; ask them to suggest one key thing for improvement. When people give feedback, document this in your reflective diary, and ask if you can follow up as your goal progresses. Gathering feedback from others on an on-going basis indicates your desire to increase your levels of self-awareness, as does your on-going reflections about your goal attempts. For example:

> "Looking at the appraisal by my placement (internship) year line manager I observed as significant lower scores given on: 'Effective management of time', 'Motivation, initiative and proactiveness' and 'Interest shown and Sustained' as three areas that I strongly agree are in need of improvement... my old school reports also fed back that I am very much capable of attaining high grades, however I lack the motivation, interest and work ethic required to reach my full potential. What's interesting is that this is not consistent with my attitude towards sport. I have always found giving 100% on the sports field very easy, even in the areas that I find less enjoyable. Work ethic is not something that usually features in my constructive feedback from coaches. Why this is not consistent with my academics I am not fully sure...but I do not enjoy the methods by which my academics are taught. With a heavy portion of book learning and a vast quantity of theory involved, I have definitely struggled to maintain focus and motivation both at school and university."

This goal setter combined the feedback from two sources and reflected on it to derive insight into their lack of motivation so they could start to work on a goal area in Stage 2.

Moment for Reflection
What feedback could you seek and from who to start to work on your personal development?
How can you ensure that it is given freely and honestly?

Now, Reflect on Life Experiences and Behaviour Patterns

When engaging in self-awareness, my goal setters find that the same themes for development crop up time and time again, through school, university, internships, etc. Accordingly, as part of Stage 1 activity, I encourage them to revisit past evidence, for example, from internship feedback and old school reports to examine which behavioural 'quirks' are still hanging around in their lives and/or current roles. Combined with other self-awareness activities, this can help them identify styles and behaviours and how they are affected by the contexts that they find themselves in. For example:

> "A common theme in my school reports was that I am "a hard worker", with the "the right attitude" and "lots of enthusiasm". Since secondary school I can agree that I have sustained a certain level of being a hard worker, when required. Especially in my job placement year. However, my study work ethic has faltered over the years causing me to become stressed due to unexpected demands and high expectations that I put on myself. The pressures to succeed, in addition to the high expectations set by myself and my educators, are increasingly higher even without delving into the growing financial burdens and consequent hardships in students. I can't help but notice my dip in work ethic since leaving the strictly structured environment of school. In terms of strict timetabling and structure, this is not completely the case for university."

> **Moment for Reflection**
> Think back to your early/school days.
>
> - What did you get praised for at school?
> - What did you get into trouble for?
> - Do these things still hold true for you?
>
> How might these reflections help you consider areas for development in your life now?

As an example, many reflective goal setters work on their wellbeing. Research has explored links between wellbeing and childhood characteristics. For example, Hampson et al. (2006) found that childhood conscientiousness influences core aspects of adult wellbeing: health, friendships, and mastery. Also, aspects of adult wellbeing are found to be predicted by childhood personality traits, such as educational attainment, career success, the quality of peer and family relationships, and antisocial behaviours (Ozer & Benet-Martinez, 2006; Roberts et al., 2007).

Consider Your Consistent Story

In addition to examining patterns of behaviour, I invite reflective goal setters to reflect on their consistent story to date and to imagine what they would like their story to be in the future. The consistency of our narrative over time, and the way others tell and retell our story, powerfully shapes the way we see ourselves. For example:

> "'Josh is a polite, friendly boy with a great sense of humour'. This is the sentiment of all my primary school reports; however, my self-concept at that time was that I was a very quiet kid. I would even have described myself as an introvert at this time. But in retrospect, when searching through my school reports, I found two flyers from dramatic productions in which I had taken relatively large roles, something I had previously forgotten. My personality is one that is naturally drawn to the stage and it seems this was the case for me. Following analysis using the concept of social comparison theory, I

(continued)

> realised that important people in my life, such as my parents always told me I was a quiet kid and I was also the quietest among my two older siblings. This made me the 'quiet one' in comparison. Local information does tend to have a higher impact on our self-evaluation than distant information and my family life was closer than my school life. Therefore, I may have evaluated myself as a 'quiet kid' because of this, even if I was not."

This is an example of the impact of others crafting a story for us that might not match the story we would want to tell. Our stories and where they originate from can be very powerful indeed (Ibarra & Lineback, 2005).

Unless we self-reflect honestly and critically, we may fail to notice the themes and patterns emerging in how we go about thinking, the decisions we make, the way we interact, and the issues we have in our interactions. What we believe to be the tale of who we are might affect how we approach life, how we view ourselves and subsequently how we choose and set goals. Reflecting on the story can help us see where we have failed to tackle areas for potential goals in the past and suggest ones appropriate for now. Stories may well linger and impact on our future roles as managers and leaders.

> **Moment for Reflection: Your Future Story**
> Ultimately, what story would you want people to tell about you/ your life (e.g., from your place of study/your family/friendships/ your career/your leadership?). For example:
>
> - Who are you?
> - Why are you here?
> - What do you care about?
> - What is your passion?
> - Do you have integrity?
> - How do you treat people?
> - What is your desired legacy?
>
> Based on those answers, what steps do you need to take for that story to be told accurately and powerfully?

NEXT, EXAMINE EXTERNAL INFLUENCES ON YOU AND YOUR BEHAVIOUR

An important part of self-awareness is assessing the impact of external factors on how we behave, think, feel, and how we see ourselves. The information we store about ourselves affects our current perceptions and is affected by both internal factors (e.g., our needs, intelligence, memories, etc.), and external factors (e.g., the environment, social media, culture). So, our behaviour is a product of both the situation (e.g., cultural influences) and of the person (e.g., personality characteristics) (Fiske et al., 2010).

Consider this further explanation from Josh regarding his behaviour:

> "High school was where I convinced myself that fitting in was very important. My particular high school had a very cutthroat culture and if you didn't fit in, you would be bullied. Here I did not take part in any drama-related activities although there were many opportunities. Unlike primary school, there was too much social stigma attached to it. I believe I fell victim to socialisation, and I thought that it wasn't something that boys like me did. It has been shown that many boys are socialised to adopt normative masculine (often homophobic) beliefs. Although I was not aware of it at the time, I believe I had an unconscious gender self-concept leading me to believe this was not something I as a man should do. I remember ignorantly saying it was 'gay' and I felt that getting involved with something like this wasn't an option."

It is important to explore the impact of external factors to gain a realistic perspective of who we are and what we are about, to enable suitable goal selection in Stage 2. For example, another goal setter reflects on the impact of social media:

> "Being a part of the group of young impressionable woman growing up through the spike of all things social media, it is not uncommon to believe certain things such as identifying your worth as the size of jeans you fit into, or the concept that cellulite isn't normal. After roughly 10 years on Facebook and 9 on Instagram, I now recognise that my presence on social media is part of my identity, however this

(continued)

identity is starting to have a negative impact on how I perceive myself. Research has shown a decrease in body satisfaction with the increase in exposure to 'Instagram vs reality' photos which showcase people in an idealised depiction and the other in a reality environment. In a more recent study, it has been said that even a brief exposure to an idealised/edited photo increased body dissatisfaction, negatively influencing the perception women have on their own body."

A nice example of the perceived impact of culture is offered by this goal setter:

"As a collectivistic culture, Romanians seek interpersonal relationships, social roles, duties and obligations of individuals regarding their group. The society's ethical values, morals and traditions originate from old times and are adapted to the contemporary world. Kindness defines me, as I grew up learning how to be helpful, generous, and considerate to other people. However, I have a hard time applying the same principle to myself as I often view and critique myself negatively."

IDENTIFY WHAT MATTERS TO YOU: YOUR VALUES

Some evidence suggests that if we root our goals in positive personal interests and values, we are more likely to succeed (Sheldon & Elliot, 1999; Sheldon & Houser-Marko, 2001). As part of enhanced self-awareness, we should identify our personal values, evaluate them, and explore how they might influence our choice of goals. When we think about *how* we want to live our life, we are focusing on values. Values are like a compass that keeps us headed in a desired direction and are distinct from goals. Goals are the specific ways you intend to execute your values. For example, being an authentic leader is a value. Gaining a promotion and increased salary is a goal. You can engage in responsible behaviour each day that may lead to achieving your goal and continue to live that value even after it's achieved.

Self-awareness is a prerequisite for self-authorship. "[Self-authorship is] the ability to reflect upon one's beliefs, organize one's thoughts and feelings in the context of, but separate from, the thoughts and feelings of others, and literally makes up one's own mind" (Magolda, 2001, p. 6). Self-authorship has cognitive, interpersonal, and intrapersonal dimensions. This intrapersonal dimension of self-authorship exists when we develop our self-understanding based on internally constructed values and beliefs, rather than based on external influences (Magolda & King, 2004). This can help us choose our goals more wisely.

Goals that flow from values are inherently more meaningful and more likely to be achieved than those picked at random or selected because we think we *should* focus on them. Take the goal of losing weight. What is behind this goal? Is it because you value fitness or self-care, or taking on challenges? Or, is it because images of others on social media make you feel bad? Understanding the value behind a goal allows you to make choices and engage in behaviours in any moment, that are in line with behaviours determined important to YOU. When the goal lacks a value behind it, then the only measure of success becomes achievement.

> **Moment for Personal Reflection**
> So how do we start to figure out what we value? Picture your retirement party and all the people who would be there. How do you want the people in attendance to speak about you—what would they say that you stand for, how would they describe what you mean to them or the role that you have played in their working life. Would they describe you as an assertive, encouraging, and industrious leader? As an authentic, caring, and respectful colleague? As a compassionate, empathic, and supportive coach? As an adventurous, creative, and curious entrepreneur?
> Values focus on HOW you want to be as you move through the moments of your life, rather than on WHAT you want to achieve.

Consider What Significant Others Need

A significant other is any person who has great importance to our life or wellbeing, and any person with a strong influence on our self-concept. The phrase was popularised in the 1980s by Armistead Maupin in his book 'Significant Others: Tales of the City'. For our purposes, we are referring to anyone who might have an interest in or be affected by our goal, our current approach to how we do things, and our personal development.

While carrying out our self-awareness, it helps to think about what these significant others might need from us—be it at work, at home, or society more broadly. What might they need us to contribute or cease to do? From this analysis, we can find an area for improvement that stands out as something that would benefit others as well as ourselves. For example, productivity, efficiency, time management are all individual goals that impact our team overall. Increased empathy, better communication, and improved impulse control might benefit our relationships with family and friends. For example:

> "My self-awareness work has highlighted to me that my tardiness with time keeping usually lets down others in any team or study group I am a member of. That bothers me now I see it in black and white, and I believe it is a crucial goal to pursue, now while at Uni, so I get to develop a better work ethos."

> **Moment for Reflection**
> What might significant others in your life need from you right now? Choose a work and non-work example.
> How might this link to a potential goal area for you?

WRITE DOWN YOUR FINDINGS

As with all stages of Reflective Goal Setting, documenting reflections and new insights gained is important. So, begin to log findings from activities at this stage as evidence to support goal brainstorming in Stage 2. Acquiring accurate self-awareness is only the beginning; true personal development requires us to take it to the next stage—selecting suitable goals. A final thought from a reflective goal setter:

> "I think the main 'active ingredient' of Reflective Goal Setting for me was the enhancing self-awareness stage. Previously this was one of the steps that I completely neglected and didn't understand its value. I feel like it allowed me to set more achievable goals by fully understanding my current situation and therefore I could set an attainable, yet challenging goal which I have always failed to do in the past."

Summary

Stage 1 required us to:

- Identify and engage with relevant self-awareness activities.
- Gather and evaluate feedback.
- Reflect on life experiences and behaviour patterns.
- Consider our consistent story.
- Examine external influences on our view of self.
- Identify what matters to us—our values.
- Consider what significant others need from us.
- Write down our findings.

References

Ardelt, M., & Grunwald, S. (2018). The importance of self-reflection and awareness for human development in hard times. *Research in Human Development, 15*(3–4), 187–199.

Ashley, G. C., & Reiter-Palmon, R. (2012). Self-awareness and the evolution of leaders: The need for a better measure of self-awareness. *Journal of Behavioral and Applied Management, 14*(1), 2–17.

Bandura, A. (1977). Self-efficacy: Toward a unifying theory of behavioral change. *Psychological Review, 84*(2), 191.

Bass, B. M., & Yammarino, F. J. (1991). Congruence of self and others' leadership ratings of naval officers for understanding successful performance. *Applied Psychology, 40*(4), 437–454.

Church, A. H. (1995). First-rate multirater feedback. *Training & Development, 49*(8), 42–44.

Church, A. H. (1997). Managerial self-awareness in high-performing individuals in organizations. *Journal of Applied Psychology, 82*(2), 281.

Cooley, C. H. (1902). Looking-glass self. In *The production of reality: Essays and readings on social interaction* (Vol. 6, pp. 126–128). Sage.

Covey, S. R. (2013). *The 7 habits of highly effective people: Powerful lessons in personal change.* Simon and Schuster.

Dierdorff, E. C., & Rubin, R. S. (2015). We're not very self-aware, especially at work. *Harvard Business Review.*

Duval, T. S., & Wicklund, R. A. (1972). *A theory of objective self-awareness.* New York: Academic.

Eurich, T. (2018). What self-awareness really is (and how to cultivate it). *Harvard Business Review,* pp. 1–9.

Festinger, L. (1957). *A theory of cognitive dissonance.* Stanford University Press.

Fiske, S. T., Gilbert, D. T., & Lindzey, G. (Eds.). (2010). *Handbook of Social Psychology* (Vol. 2). John Wiley & Sons.

Fletcher, C., & Bailey, C. (2003). Assessing self-awareness: Some issues and methods. *Journal of Managerial Psychology, 18*(5), 395–404.

Hampson, S. E., Goldberg, L. R., Vogt, T. M., & Dubanoski, J. P. (2006). Forty years on: Teachers' assessments of children's personality traits predict self-reported health behaviors and outcomes at midlife. *Health Psychology, 25*(1), 57.

Hazucha, J. F., Hezlett, S. A., & Schneider, R. J. (1993). The impact of 360-degree feedback on management skills development. *Human Resource Management, 32*(2–3), 325–351.

Ibarra, H., & Lineback, K. (2005). What's your story? *Harvard Business Review, 83*(1), 64–71.

Kruger, J., & Dunning, D. (1999). Unskilled and unaware of it: How difficulties in recognizing one's own incompetence lead to inflated self-assessments. *Journal of Personality and Social Psychology, 77*, 1121–1134.

Kuhn, M. H., & McPartland, T. S. (1954). An empirical investigation of self-attitudes. *American Sociological Review, 19*(1), 68–76.

Leary, M. R., & Buttermore, N. R. (2003). The evolution of the human self: Tracing the natural history of self-awareness. *Journal for the Theory of Social Behaviour, 33*(4), 365–404.

London, M., & Beatty, R. W. (1993). 360-degree feedback as a competitive advantage. *Human Resource Management, 32*(2–3), 353–372.

Luft, J. (1961). The Johari Window: A graphic model of awareness in interpersonal relations. *Human Relations Training News, 5*(1), 6–7.

Luft, J., & Ingham, H. (1955). *The Johari Window: A graphic model for interpersonal relations*. Los Angeles: Proceedings of the western training laboratory in group development.

Magolda, M. B. B. (2001). A constructivist revision of the measure of epistemological reflection. *Journal of College Student Development, 42*(6), 520–534.

Magolda, M. B. B., & King, P. M. (2004). *Learning partnerships: Theory and models of practice to educate for self-authorship*. Stylus Publishing, LLC.

Mead, G. H. (1934). *Mind, self, and society*. University Chicago Press.

Myers, I. B. (1962). The Myers-Briggs Type Indicator: Manual (1962). Consulting Psychologists Press.

Ozer, D. J., & Benet-Martinez, V. (2006). Personality and the prediction of consequential outcomes. *The Annual Review of Psychology, 57*, 401–421.

Ridley, D. S., Schutz, P. A., Glanz, R. S., & Weinstein, C. E. (1992). Self-regulated learning: The interactive influence of metacognitive awareness and goal-setting. *The Journal of Experimental Education, 60*(4), 293–306.

Roberts, B. W., Kuncel, N. R., Shiner, R., Caspi, A., & Goldberg, L. R. (2007). The power of personality: The comparative validity of personality traits, socio-economic status, and cognitive ability for predicting important life outcomes. *Perspectives on Psychological Science, 2*(4), 313–345.

Sheldon, K. M., & Elliot, A. J. (1999). Goal striving, need satisfaction, and longitudinal well-being: The self-concordance model. *Journal of Personality and Social Psychology, 76*(3), 482.

Sheldon, K. M., & Houser-Marko, L. (2001). Self-concordance, goal attainment, and the pursuit of happiness: Can there be an upward spiral? *Journal of Personality and Social Psychology, 80*(1), 152.

Silvia, P. J., & O'Brien, M. E. (2004). Self-awareness and constructive functioning: Revisiting "The human dilemma". *Journal of Social and Clinical Psychology, 23*(4), 475–489.

Steffens, N. K., Wolyniec, N., Okimoto, T. G., Mols, F., Haslam, S. A., & Kay, A. A. (2021). Knowing me, knowing us: Personal and collective self-awareness enhances authentic leadership and leader endorsement. *The Leadership Quarterly, 32*(6), 101498.

Sutton, A., Williams, H. M., & Allinson, C. W. (2015). A longitudinal, mixed method evaluation of self-awareness training in the workplace. *European Journal of Training and Development, 39*, 610–627.

Watkins, D., Yau, J., Dahlin, B., & Wondimu, H. (1997). The twenty statements test: Some measurement issues. *Journal of Cross-Cultural Psychology, 28*(5), 626–633.

CHAPTER 6

Stage 2: Selecting Suitable Goals

How Do We Choose the Right Goals for Our Personal and Leader Development?

Abstract This chapter will outline how to utilise the enhanced self-awareness you gained in Stage 1 to select personally relevant, meaningful, and worthwhile goals. You will develop an understanding of the key features of this stage, the rationale behind them, and the knowledge of how to choose your own personal and leader development goals and also support others with their Reflective Goal Setting.

Keywords Specific and challenging goals • Critical scenarios • Key behaviours • Feedback

INTRODUCTION

> Jessica's activities at Stage 1 revealed key themes giving her much food for thought on potential goal areas. She jotted her observations and reflections down in her reflective diary.
> One recurring theme related to a lack of assertiveness in group situations—specifically, not putting her ideas across strongly enough—if at all! She reflected in her diary that she had always
>
> (*continued*)

© The Author(s), under exclusive license to Springer Nature Switzerland AG 2022
C. J. Travers, *Reflective Goal Setting*,
https://doi.org/10.1007/978-3-030-99228-6_6

lacked the ability to be assertive with her friends which led to them getting their own way and her being left with feelings of resentment. This theme had been hanging around since her school days and had journeyed with her from the playground to her university life. She recalled her schoolteachers making attempts to get her to speak up in class—starting off with gentle encouragement, fast developing into clear irritation.

Someone in her internship company had joked in a meeting that 'It was no point asking Jessica!'

Jessica was bright and would spend ages planning and preparing for those scenarios—but was very self-conscious when it came to group or classroom situations and tended to get overlooked, over-talked, and overawed.

Exploring her feedback and reflections, she also acknowledged that she was reluctant to 'blow her own trumpet' and share her accomplishments with others. Others saw that she was naturally intelligent and capable, so often accused her of being falsely modest. This made her feel awful. Naturally introvert, she'd been brought up in an extraverted family and was regularly teased for being quiet. She knew she had always been sensitive to this—perhaps overly so.

A lack of confident communication could hold her back in her future career and relationships.

She also realised that she was very harsh on herself—rarely cutting herself any slack, as seen by words used in her Twenty Statements Test. Though tolerant of others, she was very self-critical about what she saw as her own shortcomings. She demanded perfectionism in herself and wanted to set goals that eased some of that tendency.

She was faced with several options, all seemed plausible and worthy of focus. But which one should she choose to work on first?

She shared her goal ideas with close friends, family, and her internship manager. Job applications, assessment centres, were on the horizon and working on her self-projection and impression management in group scenarios seemed apt. She believed her compassion, diligence, humility—all identified in her Stage 1 reflections—were her fundamental leadership skills. She completed many applications for jobs, with no replies inviting her to interview. There were, however, many lectures on the horizon for her to practice talking up in, also group coursework scenarios to air her views. So, she decided on a goal of being more forthcoming where she could express her views

(*continued*)

in group situations—helpful in both academic and work-based scenarios. She was not sure how to go about this goal yet, that would all become clear in Stage 3—but for now, she had a relevant, worthwhile, and potentially powerful goal area!

"It must be borne in mind that the tragedy of life doesn't lie in not reaching your goal. The tragedy lies in having no goals to reach."
—Benjamin E. Mays

Like Jessica, we should enter Stage 2 fuelled by ideas for potential goals from our Stage 1 activity. These goal ideas are based on a strong sense of self, collected from a variety of relevant and credible sources. We may choose to set multiple goals at once, but as in the illustration, we will focus here on setting one goal at a time. The pursuit of even a single goal is challenging, but each day we are typically pursuing several goals at once—most individuals report pursuing 7–15 goals at a given moment in their life! (Little & Gee, 2007).

Let's go through key features of this stage.

Moment for Reflection
Alongside the themes that have emerged from Stage 1, we can use probing questions to help us generate goal ideas and priorities:

- What one thing could you start to do today to move you in the direction of what matters to you most?
- What is the one thing about you that most people would change if they could?
- Which one thing, that you want to do, has been hanging around, unachieved, for some time?
- What is the most important problem that you could act on right now?
- What issue or aspect of you would you want to work on, but people might advise is 'too big' to tackle? Or your own self-doubt might inhibit?

These questions might help you to tap into how you would like things to be and help you start to focus your efforts to get there.

Identify a New, Specific, and Challenging Goal Area

At Stage 2, it is important initially to consider several potential goals. Reflective Goal Setting is your opportunity to (re)write your own story and so it is key that you remove restrictions, barriers, and constraints that might hinder the process. Leave all notions of 'should' or what 'makes sense' aside for now. Your consistent story might have been preventing you from believing such goals are possible, as with Josh in the previous chapter. At this stage, your goal does not need to be fully developed, that will happen later at Stages 3 and 4. For now just consider your ideas and think about how those potential goals might fit with your future plans, your passions. If you are passionate about a goal, you will be more likely to commit—to buckle down and be successful. We derive meaning in our lives from the pursuit of challenging and worthwhile goals—known in Japanese as 'Ikigai'. Many reflective goal setters report feeling energised by this stage, even before their actual goals are set. The realisation of a range of possibilities for improvement with a clear method attached is highly motivating.

How do the goal ideas fit with your values? As we saw in the previous chapter, values are personalised views or deeply held opinions that guide chosen courses of action or judgements of outcomes. Our individual set of values is a result of learning and personal experiences. Values are influenced by many things in our lives such as our family, friends, peers, relationships, communities, etc. We are also affected by the values of our chosen organisation. They may not always be the most apt ones for us, and they may change throughout our life and career. Values can be deep set, and often influence our behaviour subconsciously, so to choose the right goals we must bring these to the fore and examine their suitability and relevance.

> **Illustration from a reflective goal setter**
> 'Wow. I had initially thought that within this first diary entry I would discuss my results from five tools that measure self-esteem and personality. Having done just one, I find myself five pages into what I thought would be a relatively short exercise, and so I think I will call it a day. The entry has highlighted some potential goal areas which is exciting as prior to this, the only goal I could think of was developing my excel skills, something I now see as rather shallow and inconsequential given the other themes that have come out of the Twenty Statements Test. I have really started to get to grips with what is important to me and how my goals might move me towards realising that. Exciting times!'

As we saw in Chap. 3, 'specific' and 'challenging' are key features of Locke and Latham's Goal Setting Theory which forms the basis of how we set goals within Reflective Goal Setting. 'Specific' refers to a goal that is clearly spelled out and related to one specific area or domain. 'Challenging' relates to something difficult, stretching, and not easy. As one past goal setter remarked "How bloody difficult is it to stump up the courage to set difficult and challenging goals!" However, we don't want our goals to be impossible to attain. Also, in Chap. 3, we talked about the impact of self-set versus goals set for us by others. The Reflective Goal Setting model works on the basis that we are choosing our own goals, even if they are informed by feedback from others and link to wider organisational goals.

> **Moment for Reflection**
> Brainstorm potential goal areas for you based on your Stage 1 activity.
> Now, consider one area to focus in on and note down your thoughts and reasons as to why.

Now, Identify Scenarios Related to the Goal Area That Currently Need Improving

During this stage, we start to hone in on the specificity we need. Let us look back on the example of project manager Brian shared in Chap. 1. If you recall, he was a popular manager and seen as kind and respectful. However, he had received some feedback in a team building activity which left him rather confused. The feedback was *'Brian, you're just not assertive enough!'*

Many of my goal setters want to work on assertive communication and have had similar feedback. They may find they resent certain people in their work or friendship group—people who always seem to get their own way or take advantage of them. They first need to identify the kinds of scenarios where assertiveness is a challenge for them. It may be that they have found themselves too quick to say yes to everything everyone asks of them at work (an example of passive behaviour), recognise that they use intimidation as means of getting others to agree with them (aggressive behaviour), or avoid direct conflict but employ sarcasm to express their annoyance (passive-aggressive behaviour) (e.g., O'Donohue & Fisher, 2008).

When dealing with softer skills, especially those involving interactions with others, identifying the specific scenarios and behaviours allows us to examine consistency across varying scenarios and relationships or only in certain ones—which helps us with goal specificity. For example, when we dove down, we found that Brian wasn't very assertive when chairing team meetings and he allowed certain people to take too much of the airtime. This meant that the feedback was getting more specific and identified key scenarios where Brian could focus his attention.

Here is an example, this time related to a goal setters lack of flexibility:

> "All these goal ideas and feedback pointed to one key skill I need to work on: adaptability. I struggle to be flexible and spontaneous when change occurs. It happens especially when I set myself a logical plan and someone or something interrupts. If someone does something to upset my flow, I find it hard to let go and as hard as I try, it gets me in a mood. For example, when we make plans to meet up to do group coursework and someone doesn't turn up. I can see it happens especially when an academic task is involved.
>
> Life throws various curve balls at you but it's how you deal with them that matters and thus I have identified one of my goals: to develop greater flexibility and adaptability. It won't be easy, but at least I know what I am working on now. Others have mentioned this before, but I now have concluded myself that this is the right area for me."

Moment for Reflection
You have so far considered a goal area. Next, you must ask yourself some key questions:

- Where do the current goal-related behaviours take place?
- Who else is typically involved?
- What sorts of tasks/actions are being attempted?
- What feedback have you had related to your current approach to this goal area?
- What tends to go well and what goes less well?

Now, Outline Specific Key Current Behaviours Involved in Your Approach to the Goal Area

Over the years working with Reflective Goal Setting, I have no doubt driven my goal setters mad, because I constantly question them on their goal-related behaviours, asking: 'So more specifically, what do you do? What do you **exactly** do?' Because to set specific goals that we can put into practice and measure progress, we need to drill down to the core of our behaviours, thoughts feelings, etc. If we look back at the examples of Josh's anxiety around presenting to audiences, we can see that he started to really focus on what his behaviour looked like, how he felt, and how he reacted in that situation.

Breaking this down and being specific enabled him to see that working on his physiological reactions would be a good start. He could observe these when he spoke up and presented in public, ask others for specific feedback, and then seek to put techniques to work on those reactions.

A further example shows a goal setter reflecting on a possible empathy-related goal

"I reflected on a recent conversation I had with a friend, where in hindsight I probably should have demonstrated more 'feeling'. Although I'm an extrovert, I very rarely talk about my feelings with other people as I know when people come to me with concerns or worries, rightly or wrongly I often am disinterested (not that I'll let them know that verbally), and will perhaps listen through gritted teeth.

Recently, a housemate asked me to go for a walk, and I agreed knowing it was likely to talk about tensions in our shared house relating to his casual drug use on our nights out. He opened up that he knew he was driving away his friends due to this habit, but confided that the reason he persisted with consumption on nights out was due to unresolved issues that he was yet to fully come to peace with, namely he and his girlfriend breaking up and a death in the family. As someone who looks to find a solution to things, I told him what I thought he should do in a practical sense, saying in a somewhat aggressive way what he needed to do. It was all very matter of fact and direct, as if it were the sort of thing, I would say to myself if I were in that position ... this probably wasn't the right thing to do.

(continued)

> For him to ask me to go on that walk, it was very unlikely, at that time, he wanted to be lectured about his lifestyle choices. What I thought was being a good friend offering sound advice probably just made him more stressed about his situation, likely causing him to feel worse about himself than when we left the house. Because I don't have time for what I often would describe as 'wishy washy feelings s**t', I feel I failed in my duty to be a good friend and just listen for once instead of always trying to solve the problem."

> **Moment for Reflection**
> Thinking about the goal area you have personally identified, what EXACTLY do you do and in what scenarios?
> Really try to pinpoint the exact specific things you do.

Assess the Impact of These Behaviours on Yourself and Relevant Others (Such as Your Family, Friends, Partner, Employees, Group/Team, and the Organisation

When considering your current behaviours, it is important to reflect on the impact of less effective behaviours, attitudes, and the responses on other people.

Jessica reflected on others' responses towards her, but then reflected in depth and with honesty, which helped her see that her behaviours could result in frustration for those who loved her, the slowing down of discussion, and issues arising from her not sharing important information. She recalled studying the theory of Groupthink (Janis, 1982) and realised that she was often one of those people who self-censored and succumbed to direct pressure—which was not helpful and did not bode well for any future leadership roles she may take on. This helps us see that the motivation for our goal is often wider than just personal empowerment. A further example:

"I feel if you were to ask my friends and family for some of the more negative aspects of my personality, a common response would be how I can be very argumentative. This ties in with other descriptions of me, such as honest, knowledgeable, and intellectually curious. I believe it is through my intellectual curiosity that my argumentative tendencies arise, as I will only argue with someone if I have unwavering conviction in my own point of view, often meaning I perceive what the other person is saying as wrong or incorrect. Personally, I feel having the ability to stand up for one's own beliefs is a skill, however at times it may hinder my relationships with others and ultimately stunt both personal and professional growth. On my placement (internship), one piece of feedback was for me to better remember and understand the hierarchy of the firm. This was explained by my manager, telling me that although what I said and challenged colleagues on was often correct, the issue of an intern openly challenging a Senior Associate or Vice President was a trait that would more likely hinder my career than help it. As such, looking to influence others in a different, more diplomatic way is definitely something I could look to tie into one of my goals."

You can also examine in more depth the need for your goal from your team's perspective if you are in the workplace. How does it match the organisation's values? What is the organisational strategy and how might your goal fit in?

Moment for Reflection
What have you seen to be the impact of your current approach to your goal area on others?
What feedback have they given you about how it impacts on them?
What have been the implications?

Obtain Feedback (e.g., From Lecturers, Family, Friends, Peers, Mentors, Managers, Significant Others, etc.) on Goal Choice Where Possible

Once you have decided on your goal area, it can be helpful to run your idea past others who you trust to give you honest and supportive feedback. Avoid anyone who may have their own agenda and cannot be objective and supportive about your goal. You can ask them: how relevant do they think it is to you, do they foresee any contextual barriers, any potential support, do they think it presents you with sufficient challenge, do they think it will help you grow?

Even those of us who believe we are self-aware can benefit from asking someone else for help with our chosen goal. If you are still wavering between options, they can help you pin down the right choice, or give suggestions for implementing it correctly. They may even offer support. For example:

> "A potential goal to work on is something I wrote in my Twenty Statements Test—arrogance. I found it interesting, upon further inspection of my responses to the test, at how closely this term links to many of the positive statements I have listed, including: Confident, knowledgeable, and opinionated. The definition of arrogant; 'having or revealing an exaggerated sense of one's own importance or abilities' bears similarities to that of confident, 'feeling or showing confidence in oneself or one's abilities or qualities.' I am and have been told by my internship managers that there is a fine line between arrogance and confidence. Whilst I've never been called out for being arrogant, I think it's possible that at times people may misplace my confidence for the former. As such, when considering goals, I will keep in mind that a goal that can enhance one's humility could be beneficial in the long run. I chatted to a few of my friends and family member about this goal idea, and their enthusiasm for my goal choice suggested this was something that was important for me to work on!"

> **Moment for Reflection**
> Who could you ask for feedback on your goal?
> Think of people that will be honest, and that you can trust to have your best interests at heart and without their own agenda.

START TO FORMULATE A GOAL FOCUS AND WRITE IT DOWN!

Now that you have a goal area to begin to work on and you have given this some detailed thought, write about your ideas in your diary. You can write about how you came upon the goal idea, your reaction to it, how you feel about the feedback you have obtained, and any initial ideas for the how, as well as the why. You are not writing out the goal in full detail yet, that's for Stage 4, but it's helpful to keep logging your thoughts and ideas.

This following goal setter is all set for Stage 3 where more detailed work will be done on their goal.

> "My reflection today was prompted by the lecture on Non-Verbal Communication. Two elements of the session could contribute to my goal selection. Firstly, the insight that tone of voice accounts for 38% of non-verbal communication was an eye opener for me. A key development area that became apparent in my job placement year was to improve the way I influence people—to be less direct and patronising when responding to others. Often when someone just doesn't get what is being done, or shares ideas that are clearly wrong, or beats around the bush too much before saying what is important, I can speak back—not in a rude way—but in a tone that shows the person I am frustrated or growing impatient. Therefore, I want to work on my tone of voice when speaking to others to ensure I am not being too direct, potentially coming across as angry or frustrated. I will do further research into the impact vocalics has on interpersonal relationships and look for ways in which I can develop them to become a more welcoming and likeable teammate and friend."

Final Moment for Reflection
Further things to reflect on and write about:

- Why do I choose this goal area?
- What will it give me that my current behaviour(s) doesn't?
- How does it map onto my values?
- What do I ultimately want to achieve in the future?
- What do others think about my goal choice?

SUMMARY

Stage 2 showed you how to:

- Identify a new specific, challenging goal area requiring improvement.
- Focus in on specific past and current scenarios and experiences related to that goal.
- Outline your specific behaviours, feelings, attitudes, and thoughts currently exhibited in those scenarios and experiences.
- Evaluate the impact of those behaviours, feelings, attitudes, and thoughts on others you interact with, your team and organisation.
- Obtain feedback from others on your goal choice if and where possible.
- Start to formulate a goal focus and write it down!

REFERENCES

Janis, I. L. (1982). *Groupthink: Psychological studies of policy decisions and fiascos* (2nd ed.). Houghton Mitflin.

Little, B. R., & Gee, T. L. (2007). The methodology of personal projects analysis: Four modules and a funnel. In B. R. Little, K. Salmela-Aro, & S. D. Phillips (Eds.), *Personal project pursuit: Goals, action, and human flourishing* (pp. 51–94). Lawrence Erlbaum Associates Publishers.

O'Donohue, W. T., & Fisher, J. E. (Eds.). (2008). *Cognitive behavior therapy: Applying empirically supported techniques in your practice*. John Wiley & Sons.

CHAPTER 7

Stage 3: Visualising Successful Goal Behaviours

What Will My Goal Look and Feel Like and How Will I Know When I Am Achieving It?

Abstract This chapter will provide you with the insight to identify ideal future goal-related behaviours using visualisation, and to generate the means for measuring progress and success by identifying standards and outcomes. This will help you develop the motivation to strive towards your chosen goals. You will identify the performance gap between your future and current goal behaviour.

Keywords Visualisation • Role models • Good practice • Performance gaps • Measuring progress

Introduction

> **Strictly Goal Dancing**
>
> My first experience of the power of visualisation was as a young Ballroom and Latin American dancer entering competitions. Training for an upcoming tournament, I needed to master a particularly difficult routine. My dance teacher advised me to relax and imagine how that dance routine would look being performed by someone else. That way I could see it in action and could see how it worked, then I was to imagine my own body carrying out that routine, imagining experiencing **exactly** how it would feel in my body as I went through the routine with the music, the glides, the coverage of the floor, the pace, the awareness of my partner's corresponding moves.
>
> The key was to try to intently feel what my body would experience: the flow as I danced and switched weight from foot to foot. The sound of the music as I moved. This was bringing it in to reality and closer to the event.
>
> I went on to win that competition and became the UK's North West Gold Medallist of the year in the Rumba! (I was 11!)
>
> "The body won't go where the mind has not gone to first."—Anon

Visualisation in the context of Reflective Goal Setting is about 'seeing' our goals and imagining them being successfully executed: driven by that potential new and effective way of behaving, thinking, and feeling. Personal development is about recreating and/or refining aspects of ourselves and our behaviour. Visualisation techniques can play a part by enhancing focus and confidence and have long been used by those deemed successful in achieving their desired outcomes. Jack Cranfield is a major advocate of visualisation, defining it on his Twitter page in 2018 as '...*the technique of closing your eyes and picturing yourself enjoying life as if your goals had already been achieved—in rich detail...*' Despite claims that visualisation can accelerate our goal success and personal development, be it to establish new habits, improve our health, remove our fears of public speaking, or learn new skills, we are rarely taught how to use it effectively.

Visualisation is included in Reflective Goal Setting as many of the skills it targets have a physical and sensory element. For example, speaking assertively, listening attentively, behaving confidently and positively, and expressing calm when faced with a threat. Used properly, visualisation can physically mimic a true sensory experience without any actual external stimuli, essentially via the use of imagery. For example, many athletes employ it successfully as a technique to acquire or practise complex motor skills, rehearse routines to create muscle memory, and develop a greater sense of self-awareness to improve performance. There are several theories that explain how it works and links to personal development. One good example is Psycho-Neuromuscular Theory.

Psycho-Neuromuscular Theory, proposed as long ago as 1874 by British physiologist William Benjamin Carpenter, postulates how the use of mental imagery of an activity can improve the subsequent motor performance of that activity. During the processing of an image, the brain sends impulses to our muscles. These impulses are identical to those that cause muscle contraction with movement but are of lower intensity. The neural pathways are thereby strengthened, facilitating the learning and performance of motor skills. So, vivid, imagined events create the same neuromuscular responses as if you were having the actual experience. The more vivid and real, the better. So we should try to engage all the senses in the image, duplicate the emotions we may feel, the background activity that will be going on, the lights, smells, sounds, etc. The resultant muscular contractions are so minute that no noticeable movement takes place, but the same neuro pathway is used—establishing a 'memory' of that action. As an interpersonal example, imagine a person at work who you struggle to interact with, ask for help from, and who makes you anxious. You may well physically respond to that image even without them being present. Practising using imagery of talking calmly and clearly when asking for something from them can get our brain to interpret this as if we were making that request, providing similar (albeit smaller) impulses in the brain and if relevant, in the muscles.

So, for Stage 3, if we take an area of performance that requires enhancement, we need to firstly get a clear image of what performing that to our level of 'perfection' would look like. Then, we can repeat it again and add in sensory information (see, hear, taste, smell, or touch) and positives (strong, steady, soft, fast, etc.). The positives are what you **want** to happen.

Here is an example of our reflective goal setter, Josh, using a Stage 3 activity before we go through aspects of the stage in detail.

"Although I considered myself quiet in my early days, I always thought I was a confident individual until one event. At a school arranged employability function, I was required to do a group presentation to approximately 50 people. Before I was due to speak, I felt my heart start to beat very quickly and my arms shake uncontrollably—both typical physiological symptoms of anxiety—and when I came to speak, I froze!

I remember at that time I was focusing lots on what people were thinking of me. After this event, I lost all self-efficacy concerning public speaking and believed I was unable to cope with the challenging demands of performing this function.

Due to that bad experience, I associate public speaking with danger and appraise it as a threat due to the fear that I will be judged negatively by my peers. I believe that I do not have the skills to deal with this perceived threat and therefore avoid the situation. Through avoiding this task repeatedly, I have reinforced the perceived danger this situation holds and my inability to cope with it.

The association of danger means I experience significant cardiovascular changes, including increased heart rate and sweating, alongside hand shaking and a weak voice. The lack of control of my body is the reason I lack self-efficacy, and I have convinced myself that I will be ridiculed due to these physiological symptoms.

Ideally, I would like to set a goal to have control over my body when presenting and stop avoiding opportunities to present and overcome this perceived danger by gaining the self-efficacy to perform in this situation. My future role as a leader will require this of me.

So, I have studied some texts on how to manage public speaking, especially around breathing techniques, and positive self-talk. I have also observed how some of my best lecturers approach it and chatted to some friends who do it well and identified the gap between the ideal and how I currently do things. To develop this skill, I find a quiet time and place, and close my eyes, do some deep breathing, and visualise myself acting out the successful behaviours of presenting effectively and without the physical reactions.

Exposure therapy has been shown to be very effective therefore, I will attempt to talk more in lectures, observing my feelings and body's reaction, as well as those of others around me, as a measure of progress and feeling in control."

We will return to the goal progress of Josh later, but for now, let's look at the features of this stage in detail and build on goals you've identified in Stage 2.

Reflect on Your Previous Successes and Failures with the Goal Behaviour

It is important that we reflect carefully on any past/current attempts at the desired goal area. We may find that we perform habitual ways of thinking, feeling, and behaving and may suffer from what Freud called 'repetition compulsion' (Freud, 1914)—a psychological phenomenon in which we repeat an event or its circumstances over again. This may involve re-enacting the event or putting ourselves in situations where the event is likely to happen again.

We can also draw on Ajzen's Theory of Planned Behaviour (1991). Used to explain and predict behaviour based on attitudes, norms, and intentions. This introduces the concepts of perceived behavioural control, significant others, and intention. It can help us understand factors that prevent any changes in our behaviour. For example, do we begin with good intentions, but are affected by what others think and do, and/or don't perceive that we have the power to do anything about it, so do nothing?

As discussed in Chap. 5, when reflecting on ourselves, it is too easy to focus on our failures and weaknesses, but reflecting on previous successes is also powerful. For example:

> "I found it so much easier to study when I was at school. Arriving at university, I found it hard to self-motivate, manage my own time, and study as independently as is required. Looking back at the 'active ingredients' for success at school has shown me that the clearer structure and greater direction and monitoring from my teachers suited my character. I need to find ways of bringing some of those into my present study scenario. I don't really enjoy solitary study and prefer the classroom situation, the noise of others working around me. I am going to identify similar minded others and set up a small study/revision group. This will provide the support, stimulation, and accountability I need. Being aware of this need in me, will help me close the gap between how I studied at school and how I am studying now—i.e., less effectively."

> **Moment for Reflection**
> Consider your goal, have you had any success in this area in the past, and if so, why?
> If this has always been an area for development, why do you think that is?
> Do you repeat similar patterns of behaviour, thoughts and feelings?

Review Available 'Good Practice'

To be able to visualise effective goal behaviour we need to identify good practice. For example, you may have identified listening as an area for improvement, but don't yet have a good grasp of what constitutes good listening in practice. This is where strong psychological theory, frameworks, and models can be applied. We can draw on many sources to highlight the behaviours and approaches that we should be aspiring to, be those academic papers, self-help books, and/or online materials. Often, this is vast in nature, so a critical eye is necessary. Good theory that stands the test of time is helpful. So, for example, much literature and models on active listening, also called empathic listening, has been used by my goal setters over time. Active listening suggests restating a paraphrased version of the speaker's message, not talking too much, asking questions when appropriate and maintaining moderate to high non-verbal conversational involvement. Practitioners and researchers, including from education (e.g., McNaughton et al., 2008), and leadership (e.g., Hoppe, 2007), identify this as an important communication skill. Let's look at an example:

> "Having identified listening as one of my weaknesses from feedback and self-assessment, I knew I needed some best practice ideas for how to do it better. Finding a journal paper that said that people who were actively listened to felt more understood than those who were given advice or simple acknowledgements, motivated me to go for it. Looking back over the analysis of where my listening goes wrong in the past, I decided to work specifically on my use of questioning. I tend to be too eager to offer my own opinions, and mentally rehearse my next comments, rather than asking for more from a speaker. So, I will ask questions to encourage others to elaborate on their comments, beliefs, or feelings. This should also communicate greater empathy and builds trust."

> **Moment for Reflection**
> Consider your goal area.
> Where could you begin to look to find best practice/theory/ advice on how to improve your performance?

Observe Role Model Behaviour

A role model is a person whose behaviour, example, or success can be emulated by others. Credited to the sociologist Robert Merton (1949), the term refers to individuals comparing themselves with reference groups of people who occupy the social role to which the individual aspires. So, a manager might aspire to be a more senior leader and use a current leader as a role model. The term gained popularity in the late twentieth century but is now viewed less favourably. However, role models can be great assets when we're trying to develop key skills for professional and leader development. Stage 3 encourages us to identify role models in work or non-work settings related to our goals and specific skills. This gives us freedom to identify those who do things well, (and not so well), aspiring to specific aspects of many varied role models, rather than being subjectively and sometimes unhelpfully tied to just one coach or mentor. So, for example, we might look for someone who we know is a good listener or shows resilience. Whatever it is that we want to improve, we need to observe what they do, how they manage and express themselves, how they respond to situations and evaluate that. We may also engage in conversation with them to discover more about how they think and process things when reaching their decisions in certain situations. For example:

> "The increasing pressure in my new management role is taking its toll. I want to work on a stress-related goal and was focussing in on work life balance as an area. My colleague seems to get her work done, but also has a life! She and I are very similar in many ways, similar role, except she is a bit further along than I am in her experience and her kids are older. I invited her for a coffee, and we engaged in a frank and open conversation. We identified a couple of scenarios where the stress really hits, and I asked her about the process she goes through when deciding what to do and what to leave. I got insight into some great strategies for prioritisation, but I also realised that

(continued)

> half of my problem is that I am a people pleaser. So, if someone asks something of me, I focus on them and their needs rather than my own and the task requirements. I end up saying yes to everyone and am not delegating enough. Gave me lots of food for thought. Off to read some material on assertiveness and delegation!"

> **Moment for Reflection**
> Consider the goal area that you have identified.
> Now think of role models in your life who may already do well in this area.
> What do they do?
> How do they react?
> Could you engineer a conversation with them over a cup of tea to find out more about their approach?

Compare This 'Ideal' with How You Currently Do Things

Now that you have information about your past experiences, insight from suggested good practice, and role model behaviour, you can start to identify the variation between the ideal goal behaviour and outcomes and how you currently approach things. We can identify any behaviour that might be preventing us from achieving our goal, is not matching the best practice, and any contextual factors that might be having an impact. This also helps us start to think about ways we can measure our progress, because we now have an idea of what we are changing and what we're trying to change it to. For example:

> "Having listened to theory in lectures, read around some journal papers on the topic, observed my friend Daniel's behaviour, and compared with how I have always done things, I can see the gap between how I deal with unwanted requests from others and how I would rather be tackling it. When asked to do something I don't want to do, I usually mumble uncomfortably, apologize, and then say, 'OK then'. Then I feel resentful. I need to learn to say no. I don't need to justify my decision nor apologise. I can say no with confidence."

> **Moment for Reflection**
> Draw up a list of aspects of your ideal goal behaviour and what it will look like and then draw up a comparator list of what you *currently* do.

VISUALISE YOURSELF BEHAVING MORE EFFECTIVELY IN YOUR GOAL-RELATED SCENARIO

To perform your desired goal successfully in a real-life scenario, you need to understand what the action looks like in process. You now have a list of ways it will manifest itself. Now it is a case of picturing yourself undertaking it from a **third-person perspective**: watching yourself do it as if you are an outside observer to gain insight into the correct procedure. Then, to use visualisation effectively, you need to convince your mind that it is YOU doing the action. Here is where you see yourself doing it from a **first-person perspective** as if inside your body. The final aspect is **Intensity**, where you attempt to duplicate in your mind everything that will happen, being sensorially aware of the environment, the feelings on your skin, the smells around you, the sights and sounds—engaging all of your senses. It also helps to picture yourself in the exact setting/environment where you'll be performing this action. The more real and clear you can make it, the stronger the neuro pathways and the clearer the neurological blueprint will become. In addition, you need to ensure that you are picturing yourself **succeeding** at the action you are visualising. So, make sure that your visualisation is positive and inherently successful; the more vivid, the better.

Ways we can generate powerful visualisation might be to create a photograph or picture of yourself with your goal achieved. This is easier to access if one of your goals is something objective, such as a medal or a job title. You can then have real pictures of those things on view, on your desk—maybe even have a selfie taken with yourself smiling sagely wearing a mortar board! This is where the idea of mood boards come from—generating images to help clarify routes towards realising a potential goal. Another personal example of my own is:

> When I was undertaking my doctoral research the task seemed massive and I was struggling to envisage how it could ever be finished and achieved. Three years and submission was a long way off, so I surrounded myself with completed and successful theses and kept

(continued)

> them where I could see them while I worked. But the thing that made my fellow students laugh was the folder I created. It had dividers, a title page and acknowledgments to significant others as if it were written and about to be submitted. These activities combined gave me a clear vision of it done and dusted and successful role models to show me the way. I was motivated by the fact that it WAS possible, I could almost FEEL the sense of pride and the emotions. My approach was the same whilst writing this book!

When your goal is being performed successfully you might experience what we call 'psychological flow'. Csikszentmihalyi (1990) describes flow as a mindset that typically occurs when an individual perceives a balance between the challenges associated with a situation and his or her capabilities to meet those demands. This balance can promote flow qualities, including centring of attention, perceptions of control over actions and environment, lower self-consciousness, losing track of time, merging of action and awareness, and greater intrinsic satisfaction (e.g., Csikszentmihalyi, 1990).

> **Moment for Reflection**
> Think back to times in your life when you have achieved a state of flow.
>   What were the ingredients?
>   What were you doing?
>   What flow aspects might you be able to bring into the present to support your current goal?

IMAGINE THE ACTIONS, FEELINGS, AND THOUGHTS ASSOCIATED WITH THIS NEW BEHAVIOUR

This is where we add in the detail and vividness of the visualisation to anticipate what we would be thinking and feeling. This can add to our motivation to perform the goal. It can also help us devise measurement ideas. If, for example, we are regularly visiting the gym, how proud might we feel, how much more energy might we gain, how much more self-control? For example:

"Exam preparation always makes me super anxious. Reflecting on this I have realised this is a pattern where my emotions always inhibit my performance in exam conditions. Using visualisation to craft my goal I lay down for a while in my room, with it all quiet, and visualised arriving at the exam hall, not getting involved in any conversations with anyone as that makes me more anxious, sitting down in my seat, getting comfy, turning over the exam paper, feeling pleased and hopeful reading the questions, taking a deep breath and feeling a sense of excitement moving through my body, the quiet in the exam hall and how that is giving me the chance to think clearly and starting my exam calmly, confidently and in control—positive—strong, energized, and relaxed. It feels great!

To help me get prepared for this I have created similar conditions in my study bedroom while revising and practising exam answers to form associations with how the exam hall will be—so, no TV, radio, or social media."

Moment for Reflection
Imagine carrying out your ideal goal behaviour.
What would you be feeling?
What might you be thinking?
How appealing are those reactions and outcomes to you?

Envisage the External Feedback/Reactions That You Might Get from Others

Though it might apply to certain goals more than others, most goals will have impact on others in some way. It is useful to anticipate how others might react to our successful goal behaviour. This can be motivational, but also provides some ideas for measurement of goal progress. If, for example, we are managing stress more effectively, what would we anticipate others to do as a response? They may be more positively responsive to us, remark to us about our calmness, offer us more challenging work, laugh more around us. If we consider these responses in advance, we can use them as indicators of progress as we try out our goals. For example:

"On several occasions, my friends, my partner, assessment centre feedback has suggested I don't listen well and am not sufficiently empathic. Accepting that there must be some truth in it, I am going to work on this for my goal. I am going to seek out opportunities to speak to others and when they talk about something personal to them, rather than switching off, or verbally hurrying them along and back to the task, I will listen, and reflect back to them what I think they have said. I will use empathetic comments and with a calm voice. When I do this well, I expect that they will respond by opening up to me, not getting upset, may make more contributions in the team or group discussions, thank me for listening, display body language that shows satisfaction with the conversation etc."

Moment for Reflection
Consider your goal, what might others' reactions be if you were doing this well?
What could you look out for in others as indicators of your progress/success?

LOG THE 'PERFORMANCE GAP' YOU HAVE IDENTIFIED BY WRITING IT DOWN

All the information that has now been generated should enable you to log details of the performance gap between where you are currently and where you will be when your goal has been achieved. This information will be used more explicitly when writing up your goal in detail in the next chapter, Stage 4.

SUMMARY

Stage 3 has shown us how to:

- Reflect on our previous goal-related behaviours, successes, and failures.
- Review available 'good practice'.

- Observe role model behaviour.
- Compare our 'ideal' goal behaviour with how things are currently done.
- Visualise ourselves behaving more effectively in goal-related scenarios.
- Imagine in detail the actions, feelings, and thoughts associated with our new behaviour.
- Envisage the external reactions and feedback from others when our goal is carried out.
- Log the 'performance gap' and suggestions for measurement that we have identified.

References

Ajzen, I. (1991). The theory of planned behavior. *Organizational Behavior and Human Decision Processes, 50*(2), 179–211.

Csikszentmihalyi, M. (1990). *Flow: The psychology of optimal experience.* Harper & Row.

Freud, S. (1914). Remembering, repeating and working-through. *Further Recommendations on the Technique of Psycho-Analysis II S.E. 12,* 147–156.

Hoppe, S. L. (2007). Spirituality and higher education leadership. In B. W. Speck & S. L. Hoppe (Eds.), *Searching for spirituality in higher education* (pp. 111–136). Peter Lang.

McNaughton, D., Hamlin, D., McCarthy, J., Head-Reeves, D., & Schreiner, M. (2008). Learning to listen: Teaching an active listening strategy to preservice education professionals. *Topics in Early Childhood Special Education, 27*(4), 223–231.

Merton, R. K. (1949). *On sociological theories of the middle range [1949].* na.

CHAPTER 8

Stage 4: Formulating a Goal Statement

How Can We Turn Our Goal Ideas into Clear, Specific, and Motivational Written Goals?

Abstract In this chapter, I focus on the fourth stage of the Reflective Goal Setting model and outline the process for transforming the ideas and data gathered about possible goals from the previous three stages into a detailed written goal. Using illustrations, this chapter will help you develop an understanding of the key features and concepts that form the bedrock of this stage, enabling you to write out your own reflective goals effectively.

Keywords Specific goal scenarios • Best practice • Ethical considerations • Goal measurement • Time frame • Goal statement

Introduction

Sleeping the Goal Away

"My goal is to reduce the stress I experience, brought on by performance pressures and a perception that I won't perform to the best of my ability. Stage 1 activities highlighted my natural tendency to be a night owl, with a circadian rhythm more suited to later times of the day. My academic research shows night owls have issues with reduced attention, performance, reactions, and increased sleepiness. Detailed reflections and feedback at Stage 2 suggested I should focus on improving my sleep schedule to increase the quantity and quality of my sleep. Being a night owl is not set in stone and I can 'reset' my sleep schedule to improve control of my performance, manage my stress, and create a sustainable sleep schedule for long lasting, positive effects on my work capabilities. Other research has shown that insufficient sleep can result in increased cortisol levels, increased perceived stress from daily events, sleepiness, and unhealthy habits such as alcohol abuse—all things I suffer from. Continuity and timing of sleep are as vital as quantity and quality. Therefore, I am going to make sure that my sleep will take priority and develop routines to ensure this change becomes habitual. My friend Joe is a great role model—nothing gets in the way of him getting his sleep, and he always seems to wake refreshed, chilled, and raring to go. I visualise myself behaving more like Joe as my sleep improves rather than my usual behaviour—that is, whilst sitting and reading, lying down, watching TV, and travelling as a car passenger I experience tiredness and lethargy. I visualise feeling alert, involved, and able to converse with the driver, etc. I envisage people responding to me as a more alert 'on it' person. So, I will also monitor these behaviours in those situations as my goal progresses.

So, specifically, I will set my alarm to get me up at 7am and go to bed no later than 10 pm. I will take a book to bed to help me settle if I struggle to fall asleep. This will allow an hour to get to sleep and hopefully account for any disturbances resulting in 8.5 hours sleep each night which is the recommended sleep duration for adults. This goal will result in a long-term effective sleep schedule that will assist me to reach good productivity and efficiency during the day, reducing feelings of stress and ideally acting as an effective coping mechanism throughout my life.

(continued)

I will measure my progress in a variety of ways: My actual sleep behaviour, others' responses to my alertness, and scores on selected self-report questionnaires: The Pittsburgh Sleep Quality Index (PSQI) (Aim to improve my score by 2 points); The Epworth Sleepiness Scale (ESS) (my score is 13 'moderate excessive daytime symptoms,' and I would like to reduce it to 5 or under).

There may be times when I need to alter this routine such as on weekend nights out, or when my girlfriend visits for the weekend. I don't want to be so rigid that I affect others, as that is unfair. So, I aim to do this for 5 nights a week in the first instance. I will let others know my plans so that they can support me and encourage me to stick to my goal."

"By recording your dreams and goals on paper, you set in motion the process of becoming the person you most want to be. Put your future in good hands—your own."—Mark Victor Hansen

This illustration shows the level of detail utilised by this reflective goal setter when diarising about their stress-related goal. As we saw in Chap. 2, the power is in writing clear, specific, timely, and detailed goals for maximum impact and positive outcomes from ideation through to implementation. As discussed, there are many reasons why writing about our goals generates success, among them is the accountability it provides, the sense-making that comes from seeing things in black and white, and the added sense of purpose and direction gleaned from clearly written goals. However, there is more to it than just writing down the goal aim and action(s). Reflective Goal Setting takes us further—to fully detail all components of the goal including: what, why, how, where, who, when, and by which measurement. This is followed by on-going reflective writing of goal attempts as will be outlined in Stage 5. Many of us don't make the time to write out our goals, but the overwhelming evidence suggests that the more vividly and detailed we write about our goals, the more likely we are of achieving them. Remember the differential experiences of the two senior leaders setting personal development goals around physical fitness to manage stress and work-life balance at the start of Chap. 2?

So, don't fight it—write it!

Let's work through the key features of Stage 4.

FIRSTLY, IDENTIFY THE SPECIFIC ACTION THAT YOU ARE GOING TO WORK ON AND IN WHICH SPECIFIC SCENARIOS

As seen in Chap. 6, reflective goal setters have chosen a wide range of skill areas over the years. The possible goals are endless. In the early days of Reflective Goal Setting, interpersonal skills were the focus, but it soon became apparent that the model could benefit a whole host of soft and life skills more broadly. We may well identify a suitable goal area, but without detailed formulation, this can lead to vague and 'do your best' goals—which are not deemed to be as effective by Locke and Latham (1990). Instead, we need to drill down to more specific actions and scenarios where we want to have impact with our goals and then outline the how and when. Much preparatory work has been done before we get to this current stage, and now it is time to get that goal down on paper (or iPad, or smart phone).

Let's take an example. A reflective goal setter has discovered that they would benefit from working on assertiveness—an area chosen by many goal setters over the years, be they students, managers, or leaders. As a concept, assertiveness has lacked clarity of definition but is underpinned by a strong research base. Rich and Schroeder (1976) claim that assertive behaviour is, "the skill to seek, maintain, or enhance reinforcement in an interpersonal situation through an expression of feelings or wants when such expression risks loss of reinforcement or even punishment." (p. 1082). Whether we are students of business and management, or managers and leaders in organisations, being able to advocate for ourselves, and our teams; present our own positions, views, arguments, and objectives; handle difficult situations; be determined, but in control of (passive) aggressive impulses without harming the rights of others is very powerful. Assertive behaviour can reduce anxiety, allow for more meaningful relationships, enhance our self-respect, and improve how we adapt socially. We may be required to apply it daily.

Our prospective assertive goal setter may have investigated the effects of their behaviour when interacting with others, received feedback (like Brian in Chap. 1), observed key role models in their life, identified some links with their wellbeing and other outcomes, and completed self-report assessment inventories, such as the Rathus Assertiveness Scale (1973), and/or the Thomas Kilman Conflict Style Inventory (1974). They may have specifically identified a tendency to be passive in certain social encounters. This coupled with scrutiny of past experiences, has built a consistent 'passivity story' and led to highly relevant goal area—**refusing unreasonable/unwanted requests from significant others**.

Some of us struggle to say 'no' when people make requests of us, even unreasonable ones. We may struggle when asked to lend people money, provide constant free lifts into town, shut down cold callers, give preferential treatment at work, take on tasks and roles that are not in our job remit, etc. Our reasons to refuse are varied, we might be busy, feel insufficiently skilled, recognise we are being taken advantage of, etc. Also, some of us struggle to *make* requests of others too—being unable to ask for support, and/or seek help from others—even when it is in their remit to give it.

So, assertiveness is a good goal to choose.

A specific action therefore might be—**developing the ability to refuse requests from others when being asked to do something that we do not want to do, e.g., it will distract us from our work/study.**

From the 'Best' Practice' Behaviours Outlined as Part of Stage 3, Select Suitable and Specific Techniques and Approaches to Apply

Many strong psychological theories and frameworks are available to help us devise our goals, alongside real-life examples. Let's continue working with the assertiveness example. We can draw on theories or frameworks to find ideas for best practice (e.g., Galassi & Galassi, 1978). Studies have shown that typical features of a strong assertive personality include such things as expressing feelings openly, spontaneously, and precisely; opposing and countering others' opinions through direct and clear expression of own views; using the personal pronoun 'I' as an illustration of how we are standing behind our words and not defer to others for backing; making and dealing with requests; giving and receiving praise, not as a sign of immodesty, but as an expression of self-respect and adequate understanding of our strengths and abilities. We can examine how people have suggested we change our behaviours (e.g., Larsen et al., 2017). We can examine our non-verbal behaviour such as modulation of tone, inflection, volume, and facial expression to enable congruence with what we are saying and the given situation. We can work on eye contact, body language, maintaining an upright and strong posture, and managing distance and physical contact with those we interact with or find it hard to be assertive with (Alberti & Emmons, 1990).

Other theories can also help. For example, Berne's Transactional Analysis is extremely popular with my goal setters (Berne, 1958). We can explore the 'games that people play' and examine the impact of ego states on ours and others' behaviour in interactions. We can specify the interactions and with whom we struggle to make our 'adult' voice heard and work on reducing childlike responses and 'tit for tat' spirals (see Berne for a fuller explanation of this approach—my goal setters find it helps!).

So, we may write that we are going to—**state my response clearly and take ownership of what I am refusing, using the word 'I'. I will not say 'I am sorry,' but rather things like, 'that sounds interesting, but I am busy right now, perhaps next time.'**

IDENTIFY KEY MEASUREMENT CRITERIA TO ASSESS ANY IMPACT, CHANGE, AND PROGRESS

How many of us have said to ourselves, "I'm going to be more assertive" or "I'm going to manage stress better"? These goals are not as easy to measure as, say "I am going to get a better grade," or "I am going to improve my running speed." We can see the effect of a grade score, and we can time our speed. How can you tell how well you're doing if you can't measure your progress numerically? In a society obsessed with objective measurement, this has perhaps been one of the barriers to the value placed on soft skills—because they are harder to operationalise and measure objectively.

We can plan to measure our goal progress in several ways as we talked about in the previous chapter, both subjectively and objectively. Now let's look at this in more depth using an illustration so that we can incorporate that into our goal statement.

> Ways to measure goal progress:
> Over the years, many highly task focused goal setters have realised that they neglect spending time with their loved ones due to work/study. A popular goal-related phrase spoken by many (leaders in particular), is '*I want to spend more quality time with...such and such a body (usually family).*' This, in my opinion platitudinous, phrase is vague and rarely leads to action. Unless we state clearly what 'quality time' looks like and how we are going to measure it, it remains a vague and somewhat socially pressured declaration. How would we know if we were spending 'quality time'?
> So, we could measure it objectively for example,—'*If this goal is successful I will be spending X amount of time (e.g., an hour at a time, or a full day) with Y (e.g., my friend, Wei), it will be X often (e.g., once a day, or once a week), I will have chosen to spend time with them instead of e.g., playing golf, I will have switched off my phone/TV, we will have watched a full film without interruptions from work calls, we will have had a detailed and lengthy conversation, I will have made plans in advance and have them in my diary, and might even have bought tickets, I will not have cancelled. Afterwards, I will receive texts/messages to say thank you and what a lovely time we had,*' etc.
> Or subjectively, for example—"I will feel good and not guilty. I will have enjoyed myself. I will want to do it again. I will feel refreshed from switching off from work. My relationships will feel stronger and more connected. My reflections will be more positive. It will match my value that my family/colleagues/friends' matter."
> Do you get the picture?
>
> **What might be some possible measurements for the assertiveness goal we have been working on?**

We will no doubt experience spontaneous and serendipitous measurement once we start the process and as it unfolds, which can help us gain further insight and suggest adaptations to our approach.

CHECK OUT THE ETHICAL CONSIDERATIONS OF OUR GOAL

When considering our goals, it is important to reflect on the impact of our goal behaviour on others and consider how they might react; especially if they are to be recipients of our goal actions. Goal setting approaches are not without critique. For example, Ordóñez et al., 2009 argue that in highly target-driven organisations where people are under pressure to perform and meet organisational objectives, they may well behave unethically, cut corners, and not consider the implications of their goals. They further argue that side effects may include a narrow focus that neglects non-goal areas, a distortion of risk preferences, corrosion of organizational culture, and reduced intrinsic motivation. Though their view has been challenged by Locke and Latham (2009), it is essential that organisations and their leaders establish clear moral codes to reduce the potential for such goal-related outcomes—especially in high-stake/high-risk organisations. At an individual level, the use of on-going written reflection in Reflective Goal Setting is designed to encourage regular examination of our goal attempts in a broader landscape, gather feedback, and consider the impact on others. It is important to feed that into our goal planning—as in the example shared at the start of this chapter, when our goal setter considered the effect of his new sleep schedule of his girlfriend. It is good to also consider that our goals should not be achieved at the expense of someone else. An example of my own:

> **The Assertiveness Googlie**
> A number of years ago, I was involved with a women's management development network. We would run events and residential weekends where professionals could come along and develop skills to transfer to the workplace. For example, sometimes I would run a session on developing assertiveness—covering models and techniques and inviting attendees to set goals. My advice would always be to not 'overshoot the mark' when they returned home—rather like with the silent extrovert back in chapter one—I knew that many might go home or back to work, and try to change instantly, refusing to do this and that, bordering on aggressive as they failed to calibrate their assertiveness early on. This would throw a curved ball at their partners, families, friends, colleagues, etc. They needed to consider how their behavioural and attitudinal adaptations might affect crucial others, so as not to completely wrong-foot and undermine people they cared about.

So, in our example at the start of the chapter, he detailed **"I don't want to be so rigid that I affect others, as that is unfair."**

Provide a Time Frame/Deadline/Event

We visualised our goal in action in order to motivate and help develop measurement for our goal in Stage 3, another motivator is knowing when the goal behaviour is going to take place. We can have a fixed time frame, or an event, or it may be that we state that we will attempt our goal each time a certain event or situation occurs. That way we know the timing and duration of our efforts and have something to work towards. For example, it might be a particular project, exam, interview, or assessment centre.

Goal setters develop at different times and speeds, and some take longer to 'warm up,' taking more time to gather sufficient self-awareness, for example, whereas others hit the ground running. But unless we identify when, we are less likely to do it. As one reflective goal setter advises:

> "Reflective Goal Setting is a marathon, not a sprint. You cannot expect changes right away, you have to stay committed. At times it may feel like you 'hit the wall'. But there is a finish line. You just have to pace yourself and pat yourself on the back after each time."

Goal setters can work on distal goals, for example, *to become a highly effective leader in five years' time*. Not so easy to measure in terms of times and dates. What happens during those five years? How do you know if you are meeting the necessary smaller steps along the way? Should all goals have the same timeline? With Reflective Goal Setting, we are less interested in time as a measurable concept, but more about events. So, the distal goal becomes the vision for our shorter-term, proximal goals. It is important to feel a sense of accomplishment when you set and attain goals. Part of a comprehensive plan is to set goals that have different time frames: long-term, mid-term, and short-term. Being events led, these might not be predictable as it is more a case of seizing (or creating) opportunities when they present themselves.

> Goals and time-frames:
> **Long-term goals.** Representing major targets in your life that may take five to twenty years to achieve. Even a lifetime. Education, careers, personal relationships, travel, or financial security—whatever matches your (current) values.
> **Mid-term goals.** Representing objectives accomplished in one to five years. Such as completing a course of education, paying off a car loan, or achieving a specific career level. These goals usually support your long-term goals.
> **Short-term goals.** Are the ones you can accomplish in a year or less. Relating to specific achievements, such as completing a particular course or group of courses, taking a trip to Machu Picchu, organizing a school reunion, or developing the key skills to support these, and also mid-term and long term goals.
> It is good to have a combination of these types of goals to help identify your accomplishments along the way.

Many of the goals being set are related to habits, and 'habit' implies something regular in occurrence or routine. If we are working on habits, we can state that we will attempt our goal whenever that habit would usually be performed. For example, **to stop reaching for my phone to go on social media when I get bored. I will get up and go for a walk around instead.**

START TO WRITE OUT YOUR DETAILED GOAL STATEMENT

> "A goal properly set is halfway reached."—Zig Ziglar

This is the stage to write out the goal—not just an aim, but all the details. As we have already said in Chap. 3, the more detail the better. Certain prompts can help. For example:

"Based on my Stage 1 self-awareness analysis:
I will: work on enhancing my assertiveness.

Specifically, I will work on my inability to say no when someone makes what I deem to be an unreasonable request of me.

Try using some of my insights gained from my research, that is, Transactional Analysis—I can talk to them 'adult to adult', I don't have to be their 'parent'. I also can use Seligman's ABCDE framework—I can dispute my usual beliefs, i.e., they are not going to hate me if I say no. Also, I have observed how my other friend Ravi does this—they just say, 'I can't now but will take you on Saturday if you like, but I am busy just now.' Our other friend, James, seems to take this ok.

Need support from my friend, Sasha, who I have enlisted to give me feedback if I overstep my assertiveness and wander into the realm of aggressiveness.

Measure my progress by: their reactions, how the interaction proceeds, if they take no for an answer, how I feel about it, if there are any repercussions, how much extra time I gain to spend on my own things, and if and when they ask again.

Know I am succeeding by less agonising about it each time I do it, less resentment when I do things I don't want to, less requests.

Try this with James who does this to me all the time, and the frequent mid-week unplanned requests to take him to the supermarket when I have work to do is my first opportunity. I am going to say that I am happy to take him once a week at the weekend, and if he draws up a list for his weekly shop that will make sure he doesn't need to go again mid-week.

Accept setbacks and relish steps towards my goal! This will be like training pigeons—James is chaotic—but it's not my problem. If he gets a bit stroppy, then I just have to keep working on it and not take it personally.

Your Turn: Have a Go at Writing a Detailed Goal Statement

> **Your detailed goal**
> I will work on…
> (Identify a relevant key result area that is the performance target—decision-making, self-confidence, empathy)
> Specifically, work on… (Focus in on an aspect)
> Try using… (Identify techniques and approaches—ways you are going to carry out the goal, tools/support/techniques you might need
> Need support from… (identify others at work and/or outside of work)
> Measure my progress by…. (State performance indicators or measurement standards that specifies the targeted degree of quality and quantity to be achieved—quality of decisions, enhanced confidence, others' feedback/reactions)
> Know I am succeeding by… (A clear and desirable goal outcome outlined)
> Try this (in which scenario) and by (which date)…
> (Provide a time frame by or during which the key result will be produced—by deadline or in a week, in the following week etc).
> Write this down
> I will accept setbacks and relish steps towards my goal!

One last word from a reflective goal setter:

> "I think the key active ingredient of Reflective Goal Setting that worked best for me was having to write out my goal in detail. This made it seem more formal, rather than just an idea in my head that I could ignore. Having to formulate a strategy and write it down worked because previously I have neglected to think in detail regarding how I should go about achieving my goals. A strategy provided me with a sound starting point and more tangible activities to commit to."

Summary

Stage 4 has shown us how to:

- Identify the specific goal action to work on from Stages 1 and 2 and in which scenarios.
- Select suitable and specific techniques and approaches to apply to our goals from the 'best' practice' and role model behaviours outlined in Stage 3,
- Identify performance indicators and key measurement criteria to assess goal progress, impact, and personal change.
- Consider any ethical considerations related to our goal.
- Write out a detailed goal statement.

References

Alberti, R. E., & Emmons, M. L. (1990). *A guide to assertive living: Your perfect right*. Impact.

Berne, E. (1958). Transactional analysis: A new and effective method of group therapy. *American Journal of Psychotherapy, 12*(4), 735–743.

Csikszentmihalyi, M. (1990). *Flow: The psychology of optimal experience*. Harper & Row.

Galassi, M. D., & Galassi, J. P. (1978). Assertion: A critical review. *Psychotherapy: Theory, Research & Practice, 15*(1), 16.

Larsen, J. T., Coles, N. A., & Jordan, D. K. (2017). Varieties of mixed emotional experience. *Current Opinion in Behavioral Sciences, 15*, 72–76.

Locke, E. A., & Latham, G. P. (1990). *A theory of goal setting & task performance*. Prentice-Hall, Inc.

Locke, E.A. and Latham, G.P., (2009). Has goal setting gone wild, or have its attackers abandoned good scholarship?. *Academy of management perspectives, 23*(1), 17–23.

Ordóñez, L. D., Schweitzer, M. E., Galinsky, A. D., & Bazerman, M. H. (2009). Goals gone wild: The systematic side effects of overprescribing goal setting. *Academy of Management Perspectives, 23*(1), 6–16.

Rathus, S. A. (1973). A 30-item schedule for assessing assertive behavior. *Behavior Therapy, 4*(3), 398–406.

Rich, A. R., & Schroeder, H. E. (1976). Research issues in assertiveness training. *Psychological Bulletin, 83*(6), 1081.

Seligman, M. (1990). *Learned optimism: How to change your mind and your life*. Simon & Schuster.

Thomas, K. W., & Kilmann, R. H. (1974). *The Thomas-Kilmann conflict mode instrument*. CPP, Inc.

CHAPTER 9

Stage 5: Putting Goals into Practice

How Can We Transfer Our Written Goals into Actions for Success?

Abstract In the previous four chapters, we developed our self-awareness, identified suitable goals, visualised our goal outcomes, and produced detailed goals. This chapter will outline how to put our personal development goals into practice and will use illustrative cases. The aim is for you to gain an understanding of the stage's key features and the confidence to put your own goals into practice.

Keywords Practice grounds • Feedback • Reflective writing • Active ingredients

INTRODUCTION

> **Consulting on Listening**
> Chen was a consultant working in the UK's National Health Service (NHS). He was taking part in a leadership skills programme I was running and was about to transfer learning back to his workplace by setting a leadership development goal. He called me to tell me he had broken his leg playing squash and was unable to go into work.
>
> *(continued)*

> Determined to set a suitable goal, he picked my brains about how to do this during his confinement. Days would be spent at home with his wife while he was relatively immobile. He needed a goal that he could work on at home and transfer to the workplace later. I asked what his wife might suggest, he said listening. I asked what his team might suggest, he said listening! His character was very task focused, very introverted in style and he admitted that much of his working day was spent feeling rather irritated with those who were not as quick to get to grips with problems and tasks as he was. He knew improved listening could help him become a more inspirational leader and a better husband! So, he set a goal on 'empathic listening.' He was able to seek feedback from his wife on his efforts, but also measured her reactions to him as he attempted to listen. This went well and bolstered him for tackling his listening issues when returning to work. He reports:
>
> "On my third attempt to employ empathic listening, I started to feel more confident and found the interaction productive and positive for both parties. Feedback received after the interaction helped verify this. The process undertaken has led to a change in my behaviour when interacting with individuals in my team. The use of active-empathic listening to understand the perspectives of team members and lend context to my actions has already produced positive results in the short time it has been employed. Positive feedback so far has been rewarding, but is only the start of the process."
>
> "If you set goals and go after them with all the determination you can muster, your gifts will take you places that will amaze you."—Les Brown

Chen reported powerful transfer of learning back to his workplace with his team after honing his listening skills at home with his wife—showing there is no excuse for not practicing a goal. The skill is in identifying where it can be put to the test and then acting upon it.

Let's take another example—this time from a business and management student.

A Fairy-Tale at Christmas
Some years ago, I had a very bright and dynamic student attending my final year Advanced interpersonal skills course. He was desperate to secure a high grade in his degree, but he was aware of aspects of his personality which resulted in a bad habit of frequently starting more things than he finished. He struggled to focus and was easily distracted by a multitude of interests and ideas. He was concerned that this would affect him in his crucial final year of university and so he decided to work on a goal that had a clear beginning, middle, and end. He wanted something that he could measure objectively to practise his stamina and determination and his ability to develop a routine approach to learning.

Through reflection and his self-awareness work, he had become aware that his struggle to see things through to completion linked to his being inspired initially, but then not liking routine and the more mundane consistency of effort that some things necessitated. He identified a specific goal of consistency of effort, and he had written out in detail a goal outlining the behaviours he could attempt. He wanted to enhance his chances of leaving university with the very best grade that he could achieve. As part of his goal formulation, he identified a practice ground that was tangential to his key goal outcome, but one where he could practice seeing something through—however mundane and routine. He had always wanted to play the piano but had never made the time to learn. So, he set a goal to learn to play a tune he favoured—A Fairy Tale of New York (which has since courted some controversy over its use of particular language) by a certain time, at London's St Pancras station on Christmas Eve. The station has a couple of pianos in situ for anyone who cares to tinkle with the ivories whilst waiting for their train.

He practiced on a borrowed keyboard throughout the three-month goal setting period and recorded his regular and routine attempts on video from start to finish. On Christmas Eve, he seated himself at one of the station's pianos and started to play. When he finished a woman came over to thank him for his rendition and she was in tears. Not because of his awful playing! She explained that her husband had passed away in recent times and that it had been his favourite Christmas song. The key thing was that she recognised what he was playing and loved it!

The student went on to apply this new-found sense of self-discipline and self-regulation throughout the rest of his university studies in

(continued)

his final year. He carried out his wider reading as soon as provided by his tutors; he stuck to his revision schedule and did an amount of study each day rather than all at the last minute. He went on to realise his ambition and ultimate 'distal' goal when he graduated from university with the highest grade possible—a First Class degree! How?

- *Learning transfer*: He was able to transfer the learning from his goal by adapting and applying it to his studies more broadly.
- *Self-discipline*: Learning to play piano takes plenty of dedication and discipline. What he learnt seated at his keyboard could be transferred to other areas of his life.
- *Being held accountable*: If he had tried to do this his usual way, he may have found it too easy to put it off and not practice. Having to record his attempts both in video and in his diary, held him accountable for the goal.

This student needed to explore the levers and barriers to being routine about his efforts and motivation. Using the diary, he was able to explore this and then transfer his new insight and approach to enhance effort in his studies. He left university with a top grade after being able to apply this.

This example showcases some of the essential features of Stage 5. That is, we can practice our goals in similar situations, we can kick-start our goal setting, the benefits from the process can be non-specific, but we can also practice directly in the scenarios we are aiming for.

Many of us attend educational courses and training programmes to enhance our personal and leadership development. We may also attempt to make development plans, or seek improvement more casually by setting New Year's resolutions. The critical element is engaging in goal-directed behaviour. As we identified in Chap. 3, many of our intentions will fail to lead to desired outcomes. However, the features of the previous four stages showed us how to begin to translate our goal intentions into successful actions. A fundamental aim of Reflective Goal Setting is securing a propensity for goal setting across a range of skills and behavioural areas. Stage 5, therefore, is not a final stage as such, but rather where we try out our goals, adapt them, and if necessary, deal with setbacks, review, and gain momentum for on-going and future goal setting. Putting goals into practice successfully can lead to further gains in self-awareness, self-efficacy, and a growth mindset to begin the cycle again with a different goal. Reflective Goal Setting can become our preferred 'go to' approach to personal and leader development.

Let's look at the key features of this stage:

IDENTIFY 'PRACTICE GROUNDS' FOR YOUR NEW BEHAVIOURS/ACTIONS

We need to seek out specific opportunities for practice of our goals. Practice grounds typically refer to an area where people prepare for sporting competitions with activity providing concentration on these skills and fitness and where military personnel are trained for combat. Finding practice grounds for some skills, such as practising rapport building for an interview situation, might seem rather easy. But what if there are no interviews on the horizon? Reflective Goal Setting encourages us to identify tangential scenarios where behaviours can be rehearsed to build confidence for the later full-blown situation. Also, we need to seize opportunities as they present themselves. For example:

> "Diary entry 5th September: I didn't end up trying the bedtime meditation as I felt whilst working yesterday afternoon that the perfect moment arrived to try it when stressing out. It was good though, that whilst feeling stressed, my thoughts turned to calming down with meditation and I do feel that this habit is developing with the resultant calm being the reward."

With many types of goals, we are facing real people in real situations—and it is often hard to practice these out of the spotlight. Our goal may be behavioural, attitudinal, emotional, and/or psychological. Some goals can take place behind closed doors, others in full public view. For example, some students have worked on their confidence and talked positively to their reflection in the mirror each morning rather like a 'backstage' self, preparing for the role, before dealing with others in the 'frontstage' (Goffman, 1959).

Practice can mean perfect but not always along the developmental journey. Stage 5 considers that behavioural change and personal mastery (Senge, 1990) may take time and will depend on learning opportunities and consolidation—not necessarily hitting the mark upon the first attempt.

For example:

> **Building Rapport One Step at a Time**
> Looking at entries over time in a diary can help the reflective goal setter see improvement and the amount of *'getting back in the saddle'* that is required when working on goals. This reflective goal setter was working on building rapport in social interactions, something they found extremely hard. They report in their diary:
> "7th April—Although the interaction didn't last for long, I felt extremely self-conscious and uncomfortable talking in front of the rest of the group and it was later pointed out to me that I went bright red when attempting to speak up. The experience has decreased my confidence levels when communicating and as a result I am not looking forward to trying to put this goal into practice again tomorrow.
>
> 8th April—Although I found it difficult to hold a conversation at length, I did manage to say 'hello' or 'good afternoon' to many of the walkers who passed us, and surprisingly they responded. Although it was an effort to try and speak to others and at times, I felt stupid, each time I got a response made me a lot more confident."

WRITE TIMELY GOAL REFLECTIONS IN YOUR WRITTEN REFLECTIVE DIARY

Goal setters report that a key active ingredient for them during Stage 5 is writing reflectively about their experiences as they occur. As outlined earlier, it is important that writing takes place as close to the goal attempt as possible to reduce the chance of retrospective bias. Regular writing can have an impact, but the writing that takes place as part of Reflective Goal Setting seems to have a powerful impact because people write extensively. There are many reasons why that is the case, as outlined earlier in Chaps. 3 and 4. One reason may be due to having the opportunity to look back on situations and measure progress, another because we can examine how our initial reluctance to try things out eventually led to beneficial outcomes via our goals. For example:

> "Goal success is evident, noting that I feel in control of my time eleven times in my diary compared to once when I didn't. Diary entries 4th, 13th and 27th November display better time management by utilising problem-focused strategies from successful planning techniques to deflect stress and gain back the control I felt I had lost."

Writing, therefore, can act as a motivator to some extent and it is a way of generating our own feedback without having to source feedback from others. We can also log any external feedback we get, spontaneously or solicited, regarding our goals. Goal setters do not always hit the ground running with their reflective writing which is why it is important that people start to log their thoughts on their goals early in the process—even before goals have been formally set.

Re-adjust Goals to Accommodate Learning from Practice

Once put into practice, it may become evident that we have chosen the wrong goal or set our bar too low or too high. Perhaps we worked on a goal suggested by someone else, despite being encouraged to set self-concordant goals. There are many reasons why a goal may need to be adjusted and reflecting enables goal learning to take place, ensures its application, and reveals new self-insight gained. The on-going reflection stops us beating ourselves up if we are not hitting the mark. For example, two illustrations from reflective goal setters:

> "Starting to face some difficulties with my fitness plan, and I worry that my goal of 5 kg in a month was maybe a bit too ambitious. The problem is there are a lot of changes going on, what with having a part-time job and still trying to get back into the swing of university, and I find I often comfort eat to make myself feel better, which means that the weight loss hasn't happened."

And another:

> "I am still focussing and doing well in my meditation and tracking my emotions on a regular basis, and I do feel a lot calmer and have barely any stress when comparing myself to this time of year in previous semesters. I think having this type of strength at the moment is a lot more relevant to me than building physical strength, as body image and self-esteem can improve body confidence, so have been practicing yoga, meditation and building my mindset to be more positive—which was called 'flourishing' in the positive

(continued)

> psychology lecture. Therefore, I am going to change course with this goal a little bit and be realistic in that I will probably focus more on building and shaping my mindset rather than my body at the moment for my mental wellbeing, however, still actively try to adhere to the fitness plan."

Review Measurement Criteria

Sometimes the measurement we are using is not delivering what we need, and as we adjust our goals, we might need to refer to something more specific, such as using a measuring scale or seeking more focused feedback. We can also compare measurements from the start of the process at Stage 1. Personal Growth is just that; personal, so we are the best judge of how we have grown. Using a range of measurement metrics are best to prevent expectational and perceptual bias. For example:

> I started off monitoring my moods using a sheet that had a scale with different expressional faces from happy through to sad. I had a great chat with Mum about how I am going to measure my goals and I have decided that as of now I am going to rank my self-esteem and listening out of 10 each day.

The diary itself can evolve to become a way of measuring, for example:

> "The biggest difference for me and my progress was when I started to truly reflect in my diary. I was trying out my goals and writing out my thoughts, but what made a big leap for monitoring my progress was when I started to write in a truly reflective manner—What went wrong? What went right? Why? Is there anything I could improve on? How has today's attempt been different to yesterday etc? How have others reacted to me? What words am I using to express what I think?"

Altering how we measure our goal progress can often lead to the realisation that there has been personal change, we have just not been looking for it in the right places.

Consolidate Learning and Record Changes to Self-Insight

An important feature of Stage 5 is for goal setters to incorporate their learning into their sense of self and reflect on what that means and whether cognitive dissonance is occurring.

Some of the biases goal setters hold about themselves are debunked by their goal setting successes. For example, this goal setting manager realised they could manage time far more successfully than they initially believed possible.

> "The goal of prioritising work has been very successful in the main although I have found it difficult to not become involved in the day-to-day distractions when I am in the office. I have found that I am the most productive first thing in the morning and because I have a clear prioritised list of tasks, I have saved time that was spent each morning working through the tasks that I needed to complete. Further to this I believe I have become more customer focussed as I have found that I have been able to prioritise the tasks that are linked to customers over and above tasks that are internal and would previously have been easy distractions."

This final-year student realised they did like exercise after all!

> "The impact of exercise can be seen in my diary when I started to anticipate and look forward to exercising. The effects of exercising, being fitter and healthier were also contributing to my feelings of well-being. It was a shock to realise that I am someone who can enjoy and benefit from exercise! Who'd have thought it? Certainly not me!"

Consider Setting a New Goal!

We do not have to set a new goal immediately after achieving one but when faced with transitions, or new scenarios where we may have to ratchet up our skills or when facing a new or increasing demand, we can revisit the model and apply it to a new goal. But this time, we have our newly developed self-insight. For example:

> "Feeling good this evening. I had an opportunity to start to work on a new goal of caring less what people think today. In the gym I went to take my shoes off to do a squat (a technique recommended by a friend). As I went to take my trainers off I realised I was wearing relatively embarrassing socks. I was wearing socks that had Santa Claus on (in the middle of October) which say "I'm on the nice list". At home I would not care about this at all. However, in the gym surrounded by big alpha males, I felt apprehensive for a few seconds and thought about the possibility of people laughing at me. However, I then considered that caring less what people think was a potential new goal for me and basically said 'screw it' to myself. I took my shoes off and squatted with Santa socks on, relatively happy that I took this small step to more freedom."

KEEP WRITING!

Not everyone embraces diarising. It can be seen by some, as somewhat of a chore and the routine required, does not appeal to all. It can be challenging to write about emotions and reactions and remembering to document goal attempts and outcomes can seem onerous to some. However, very few people over the years of using Reflective Goal Setting have disagreed that reflective on-going diarising was not helpful or an active ingredient in their goal progression and success. For example:

> "The most active ingredient I would say is the diary keeping…The diary helped me open a door towards becoming more open about my struggles as a coping mechanism…I could write about it, learn how to change it, and work on it from there. This also applied to the things that I was doing wrong, such as understanding where I make impulsive spending decisions. It put into perspective how positive changes can be made and I acted on them from there."

Let's revisit the story of Josh, who set himself the goal of enhancing his public speaking:

In this example, our reflective goal setter seized an opportunity as it presented itself. This event had not been outlined in advance at Stage 3; it

"I feel I have overcome my fear of public speaking. My eureka moment came in the lecture on Transformational Leadership and Cheryl was talking about transformational speeches. She asked for a volunteer to come to the front and read out the 'I have a dream' speech by Martin Luther King...Despite feeling scared, I believed I could control my body after my work on my goal and practicing the breathing techniques and therefore felt I could do it. I put up my hand and went down to the front and read.

Grabbing the chance to do this when the chance became available, completing it successfully, I had proven to myself that I was capable, and my anxieties subsided.

I believe it was the whole process of Reflective Goal Setting that enabled me to succeed in this goal. Firstly, self-reflection allowed me to become aware of the source of this anxiety. I then visualised the successful behaviours of conducting research and exposing myself to the feared situation, setting a clear goal based on this. Finally, the process of continuous self-reflection through diary-keeping meant I was able to reflect and adapt my behaviour. Through this, I was able to achieve a goal I previously thought "would be impossible".

just required his motivation to grab the chance to practice the goal in this challenging situation. I was there to witness this, and it was very moving. When Josh put up his hand to volunteer and ventured down to the front of the class to read out this powerful speech, I felt such pride. I watched him subtly take a deep breath and 'centre' himself before starting to read. The class went quiet as they also knew this was an attempt at his goal. As he came to an end, they gave him a round of applause.

It was truly a lump in the throat moment in the history of Reflective Goal Setting!

Moment for Reflection
Where can you make the first attempt to put your goal into practice? Draw up a list of potential 'practice grounds' and commit to writing reflectively after each attempt at your goal.

SUMMARY

In this stage, we have learned how to:

- Identify practice grounds.
- Write timely goal reflections.
- Readjust goals following learning from practice.
- Review measurement criteria.
- Consolidate learning and record changes to self-insight.
- Consider setting a new goal.
- Keep writing!

REFERENCES

Goffman, E. (1959). *The presentation of self in everyday life*. Anchor Books.
Senge, P. (1990). *The fifth discipline*. Doubleday.

PART III

Practical Applications of Reflective Goal Setting

CHAPTER 10

Reflective Goal Setting for Managing Stress and Enhancing Coping

How Can the Model Help Students Manage the Stress of Their Final Year of University?

Abstract Many reflective goal setters have chosen to work on stress-related goals; successfully developing skills to cope with the pressures of university and take forward into their working lives. This chapter focuses on the experiences of final year business school undergraduate students and shows how Reflective Goal Setting can be used successfully in the management of stress and development of effective coping.

Keywords Stress • Wellbeing • Coping • Resilience • Appraisal Theory

INTRODUCTION

> **Getting on Top of Stress the Reflective Goal Setting Way**
> "The biggest difference for me since using Reflective Goal Setting is how I am now able to manage stress better and remain positive in potentially negative situations: job rejections or problems with coursework. Since setting my stress-related goal, I believe I am more
>
> *(continued)*

> resilient, acknowledging that there is more to life than just getting that job or high grade. Writing the diary helped me explore my thoughts and feelings and come to my own realisations about which goal to set without others having to lecture me on learning how to 'chill' (which, incidentally, always just winds me up and makes me more stressed!). I am not positive all the time, but I can now control my responses to some key situations, no longer letting them bring me down. Exploring the variety of ways that I coped poorly with stress, I was able to identify and choose ones that suited me and get those down on paper—never having been able to do that successfully before and always trying what I was TOLD by others would be helpful, although challenging, visualisation helped me believe I could make the changes. Activities, such as exercise, going for a walk, or painting work best for me and seeing the evidence of the impact of these in my diary, how I feel each day, and feedback from others confirms that I was right to work on balancing work and relaxation to remain positive."
>
> "There are thousands of causes for stress, and one antidote to stress is self-expression. That's what happens to me every day. My thoughts get off my chest, down my sleeves and onto my pad."—Garson Kanin

The above illustration shows how the process of Reflective Goal Setting can help students manage stress. This has always been a popular goal area for final year students, and many have tackled stress over the years using the framework.

My early research investigated occupational stress in a variety of work groups, but especially teachers (e.g., Travers & Cooper, 1991, 1993, 1996). However, my main driver was to find ways to help people strengthen their personal resources by developing effective coping skills and strategies. Reflective Goal Setting was influenced by several key stress-related theories, especially the Appraisal Theory of Lazarus and Folkman (1984). They suggest that when faced with a challenge, we primarily appraise the challenge as either threatening or non-threatening, and secondarily in terms of whether we have the resources to respond to or cope with the challenge effectively. A perceived lack of capacity or control may result in passive emotion-focused coping, such as engaging in wishful thinking—this is less effective, as it relies on short-term distractions rather than removal of the stressor. Perception of available resources typically results in active problem-focused coping, such as seeking out support from someone—which is more successful as it aims to remove the stressor. Reflective Goal Setting develops active-constructive problem-solving approaches by enhancing self-awareness, developing goals, employing suitable strategies and techniques, and engaging in on-going monitoring and written reflection. It aims to develop our personal resources which affect how we appraise events (present and future) as stressful or not, how we subsequently cope with them, and then build our resilience (see also Bakker & Demerouti, 2016, for work on Personal Resources). Reflective Goal Setting helps us identify our own (lack of) personal resources and develop our capacity to set goals—utilising a range of accompanying resources as and when required—especially during challenging, adverse, and transitional times.

Coping consists of motivational, cognitive, and behavioural efforts, enabling us to manage stressful demands and helps create the conditions needed to allow us to progress towards outcomes that we seek. Goal setting aids self-efficacy (Bandura, 1989), which in turn improves coping. Previous studies have shown that self-efficacy enhances the response of university students to study demands which may reduce harmful stress with self-efficacy playing a significant role in assessing and coping with threatening or challenging situations (e.g., Luszczynska & Schwarzer, 2005).

Working with university students closely, I observed their vulnerability to stress and their corresponding lack of effective coping strategies. Research by others reinforced my observations reporting high numbers of students experiencing stress at moderate to serious levels (e.g., Abouserie, 1994; Durand-Bush et al., 2015). Students are shown to display significantly higher levels of psychological distress, depression, anxiety disorders, physiological symptoms, and lower levels of satisfaction than members of the general population (e.g., Reddy et al., 2018), and even highly stressed occupations such as teachers and nurses (e.g., Cotton et al., 2002; Dollard et al., 2001). High levels of distress can be linked to underachievement, and subsequent effects on future careers. The start and end of the first semester can constitute the riskiest periods for negative stress-related consequences (Pitt et al., 2018), with major stressors arising from academic, financial/work, personal, family-related, interpersonal, (lack of) social support, university/life balance and starting university (e.g., Tofi et al.,

1996). Students also play a part in their own stress experience and have been found to engage in a range of unhealthy behaviours, such as alcohol consumption and drug taking (e.g., Webb et al., 1996). In addition, studies have examined the positive impact of certain personality factors, such as '*grit*' (e.g., Kannangara et al., 2018) defined as the "perseverance and passion for long-term goals" and involves "working strenuously towards challenges, maintaining effort and interest over years despite failure, adversity, and plateaus in progress." (Duckworth et al., 2007, pp. 1087–1088). Reflective Goal Setting aims to enhance qualities such as grit by developing the propensity to set goals.

So, students are worthy of study, and it makes sense for us to help them develop effective coping strategies to employ during their university days and beyond in their future careers.

Let's look at how Reflective Goal Setting can improve students' management of stress and coping stage by stage, and using illustrations from students attending the Advanced Interpersonal Skills course outlined earlier in the book.

STAGE 1: ENHANCING SELF-AWARENESS OF APPROACH TO MANAGING STRESS

Self-awareness activities are fundamental in helping students gain insight into the causes of stress, (in)consistencies in their responses, and current coping strategies. For example, do they experience differential responses in study and work scenarios? Written reflections on their self-insights as they unfold enables the formation of personal 'conceptual models' of the relative importance and interaction between the stress they experience and the role they themselves play. The greater clarity of thought acquired can lead to a more balanced and realistic appraisal of the situation, emotional recognition, and acknowledgement of the end goal. For example:

> "Over-thinking when met with a negative stimulus can often lead to a spiralling negative effect in my life-satisfaction and self-esteem. A common cause of personal distress is my inclination to overload myself with work and, in addition to anxiety around my medical health, frequently self-diagnose illness and an inclination to overthink. I am guilty of obsessive behaviour and have an inability to rationally interpret real or imagined bodily sensations as anything other than indicative of illness."

Students reflect on past experiences, behaviour patterns, and their consistent 'stress story,' gaining insight into their usual approaches to stress and coping—effective and non-effective, and how others might view their actions. For example:

> "My coping mechanisms recently have been ineffective….the crying, getting angry, not sleeping and not relaxing enough… Looking back on similar challenging periods in my life, I coped very well during my school examinations…granted I didn't have all the problems at home that I do now that cause me to worry, and my self-esteem was higher… but I also developed a very detailed timetable with my friends, which I then stuck on my wardrobe door so I could see it every day and I got great satisfaction ticking things off when I had completed them. If my school friends could see me now, stressing and out of control, I doubt they would believe it—not how they see me at all."

Feedback from trusted and significant others can also be reviewed, gathered, and evaluated alongside findings from own observations and self-assessment tools and questionnaires, related to the management of stress, coping, and stress-related effects. For example:

> "My internship manager fed back to me that I appeared anxious when asked to do something unexpected and away from my plans. Reflecting on my life to date, alongside some of the personality tests and measures, I can see that 'stressing out' when my plans go array is a consistent pattern for me. My girlfriend also confirmed that, yes! This is me!"

Documenting enhanced self-knowledge can also help with feelings of being in control and gaining belief in the possibility of success with subsequent goals, that is, developing self-efficacy. For example:

> "Regular reflective writing about who I am is starting to help me feel less stressed. It's strange… I feel more in control by examining my various personality traits, ideas, logging how I feel in certain situations. I'm starting to see things more in perspective and gaining a clear understanding of the way I behave and why, is having a very calming effect. And that's before I even start setting a stress-related goal!"

Students can also evaluate how their approach to stress relates to their values and what matters to them and others in their lives to build a basis for goal ideas in Stage 2. For example:

> "Seeing my stressed behaviour written down in my diary has made me realise how irrational I can be…this has previously caused regrettable relationship issues, particularly with ex-girlfriends. It matters to me to have good relationships in my life…and has encouraged me to address this."

Stage 2: Choosing Suitable Stress-Related Goals

Following on from enhanced self-awareness, students then identify a range of potential stressors, and prioritise a specific, challenging goal. Details of the types of stressors they report can be found elsewhere (Travers, 2011), but alongside assignments, preparation for exams, key career decisions, and associated job applications, students experience additional life pressures, such as issues with relationships, health concerns, and juggling study with part-time working. Let's take one popular example, time management, which many students report as an issue and scholars have also identified as a challenge. For example, Schuler (1979) reported that students who perceive having control over their time, report significantly better evaluations of their performance, greater work and life satisfaction, less role ambiguity, less role overload, and fewer cases of somatic tension (e.g., physical anxiety-related responses like fatigue, pain etc.). Many report they struggle to balance study demands with those from their social life, job search, and part-time work, etc. Others, just struggle to get down to work for whatever reason. For example:

> "My usual strategy when dealing with work I find too hard and stressful—I procrastinate! I felt very sure that this was the goal for me but was putting off deciding (ironic!). Spoke to my parents and they laughed and said this had been an issue since my school days! Supposedly, I'd do ANYTHING to avoid doing maths homework. I remember maths really stressed me out!"

These goal ideas are often shared with significant others at this stage and, as in this example above, they obtain feedback on their suitability.

Students also explore the role other factors may play in their experience of stress, such as their own character. For example:

> "Due to high levels of anxiety and OCD, I tend to catastrophise. For example, I have a belief that if I stop working then I will fall behind, leading to a failure in exams. So, I struggle to take breaks and manage my study-life balance."

STAGE 3: USING VISUALISATION FOR IDENTIFYING EFFECTIVE STRESS GOAL BEHAVIOURS, TECHNIQUES, AND MEASUREMENT OF PROGRESS

Using the key features of this stage, students specify the ideal behaviour, thoughts, and feelings evident when stress is managed effectively. Drawing on any past successes, seeking out role models and/or familiarising themselves with good practice from theory/self-help books, etc, they can collect ideas for effective ways of managing and coping with stress. For example:

> "I observed my mate Jack and watching how he operates gave me some good tips on how to react when the pressure hits. One of these is that when he starts to feel pressured, he goes to the gym. He says that physical activity helps get all the tension out and stops it building up and getting out of hand. That beats my approach of heading for Netflix box sets, chocolate and beer!"

Visualising the ideal future behaviour (and accompanying actions, feelings, and thoughts of themselves and others), whilst moving towards more effective strategies for managing stress, helps them document the stress-coping performance gap. For example:

> "I visualise myself having more spontaneity and flexibility. I imagine myself having a break and feeling calm and in control and refreshed. I imagine others being more relaxed around me as a consequence."

Measurement of progress can be anticipated and deemed possible. This means that stress goals are not vague but clearly constructed. For example:

> "I am going to measure my progress by seeking feedback from others on how I manage pressure, note the times I start difficult tasks rather than avoid them, and have devised my own mood-ometer based on established mood scales from the literature."

STAGE 4: WRITING OUT DETAILED STRESS GOALS

This is best demonstrated with an example:

> "I have explored mindfulness and its methods as a positive psychology intervention, to improve my management of stress. A course mate has had great success with it, and I can see the benefits for them. I will engage in the mindful activities of yoga, mindful reading and cloud watching outdoors three times a week (depending on the weather). As sleep is an issue for me when stressed, I will evaluate my success by monitoring my sleep pattern using my smart watch FitBit sleep tracking function which measures heartbeat, giving an evaluation of sleep quality and length. I will also be logging a daily stress rating, with 5 being very stressed and 0 being not stressed at all, this will be accompanied by a comment and tracked against the mindful activities carried out that day, to distinguish the effectiveness. A further measure will be if I start to see a correlation between participating in mindful activities and experiencing reduced stress levels and a better quality of sleep. I will seek on-going support and advice from my course mate."

Making time to write out a detailed stress goal is more likely to lead to successful outcomes. For example:

> "The biggest change I've seen in myself is a reduction in my stress levels. Dealing with stress is something I have struggled with for a very long time and never really improved on. By formulating a specific goal that I had to commit to regardless of any obstacles, I was forced to work on this, and it did not get neglected."

Stage 5: Putting Stress Goals into Practice and Writing Reflectively About Them in an On-going Manner

By identifying practice grounds, then acting on them, supported by clear strategies for action, and accompanied by writing timely goal reflections, students face stressors head-on. They can re-adjust/refine their goal following learning and a review of measurement criteria where necessary. They consolidate their learning and record advancement in self-insight. For example:

> "I have experienced success from implementing yoga into my routine, enabling me to reach a peaceful and calm state, which has translated into a more positive mindset, especially when faced with stressful academic situations. I have also tangibly noticed this success through a decrease in my overall resting heart rate."

One of my favourite memories of a student setting a successful stress goal was in the formative years of the model's development. She worked on positive thinking to enhance her ability to manage stress induced by anxiety-provoking scenarios: in her case, exams. She achieved great success with her goal objective of managing exam stress, but the icing on the cake was when she messaged me at the end of the summer after graduation from university. She shared how she had transferred her learning beyond our work together. The thoughts of her divorced and largely adversarial parents in the same auditorium for her graduation ceremony and subsequent celebration, and how this might ruin her day, was stressing her out. So, she employed her new skill for positive thinking and used graduation as another practice ground. She reported with joy how well the day had gone. She had thoroughly enjoyed the afternoon, and her approach seemed to have a soothing effect on her parents who took her lead, put their grievances to one side, and enjoyed the day too.

At this stage, goal setters are encouraged to write regularly and reflectively about their goals as they make attempts. I talked about the effects of writing about our goals in Chap. 3, but here I will focus on the benefits for stress and coping through writing reflectively about our goals.

The Impact of Writing Reflectively About Our Stress Goals

In addition to the benefits of writing out detailed stress-goals, on-going written reflection in a diary has been very powerful for my goal setters when dealing with stress and is seen by many as an active ingredient for stress goal success. There are many reasons why, and I have outlined these in more detail elsewhere (Travers, 2011), but here I will focus on some of the most cited reasons by students.

The Therapeutic Impact of Writing About Stress Goals

Putting thoughts and feelings down on paper appears to calm some students and helps them focus—in an almost meditative way. In this safe environment, they can explore and are creating regular feedback for themselves which is nurturing and supportive. They accept that some degree of 'unpacking' of issues takes place with certain deeply rooted aspects brought to the foreground. Often, things get suppressed when more pressing concerns take over. But writing enables them to adapt and adjust their goals for good effect. For example:

> "Writing my diaries when goal attempts happened enabled me to reflect on the raw emotions that the situations provided. The fact that I had these entries that showed progress and some that showed steps backwards, I was able to analyse what more needed to be done after each week and where I needed to focus my energy."

My findings with students working with written reflections on their stress goals support the work of Pennebaker and others referred to in Chap. 3. Pennebaker and Seagal (1999) suggest that disclosure through writing helps us make sense of our life experiences, pulling together otherwise fragmented stories, memoirs, and experiences.

My goal setters benefit from their extensive and on-going reflective writing. I am yet to assess the impact on more objective measures of stress, but the perception of its impact is well documented by students. Though, in the main, the research on diary keeping has revealed the benefits of writing about traumatic or stressful experiences on physical and psychological health, these diaries support Burton & King's (2009) findings on the use of writing about positive feelings and scenarios. Some diarists appear to have learnt the importance of making notes of the positive events that take place, so that, on later reflection, they remind themselves of what is possible. This also forges the link between a particularly useful act and a positive feeling. For example:

> "A Eureka moment was on the 10th of December when I realised that I was actually achieving my stress management goal. One quote from my diary that really stands out is 'However, I didn't get stressed! This is insane, it doesn't feel real…' You can see how surprised I was. Although I had been making gradual progress, not getting stressed about my exam timetable was a ground-breaking moment for me. It was where I really realised that this Reflective Goal Setting process was working. It was achieving something that I thought was impossible after many years of failing."

The Motivational Impact of Seeing Change Written Down

Documenting progress means frequent and even daily observation of change, which can have a positive, affective impact and motivational effect. Good and bad aspects can be seen, side-by-side, and the recording of positive experiences and emotions, alongside the negative, can lead to a surge in the desire to forge ahead and try out new strategies. This can have powerful effects and some students suggested that they would continue to use the diary approach in the future. Recording reflections in an on-going way also helped shape their experiences. Writing reflective diary entries, as goals progressed, created a set of evidence-based action researchers. For example:

> "I'm really pleased with myself, it's good that I have to write this down because it is helping me to make positive mental links between being more confident and this impacting things like speaking to new people and positive experiences, so that in the future I am even better able to challenge negative thoughts."

The Issue of Ownership of Progress and Accountability

Working on goals for an extended period and having to report back on goal attempts regularly, means getting 'back on the horse' even after a coping attempt has backfired. This, then creates a sense of accountability. Goal setters claimed that keeping a diary this way helped keep stress levels under control. In the diary, ineffectual attempts at coping can be seen clearly, as students review and reflect on the outcomes. But rather than becoming overly self-critical, their self-perceptions are mediated through their on-going goal reflection, helping them gain self-acceptance and encouraging them to feed-forward with vision and confidence for future encounters with stress.

> "As a person, I generally am blinded by how far I have got to go and forget how far I have come. Using a reflective diary encouraged me to look back at my efforts to see if these were really working. In times of success, I was able to build on behaviours to take the next step in reaching my goal. When I had come to a hurdle, I could re-evaluate my efforts and take a different path if required."

SUMMARY

Reflective Goal Setting helps students:

- Gain in-depth self-awareness about the nature and impact of stress enabling fresh insight, sense-making, and acceptance of the need to act.
- Make suitable stress-goal choices, and discover appropriate strategies and techniques to apply.
- Visualise potential outcomes of effective coping and generate ideas for measurement of progress-enhancing commitment to act on their stress.
- Target a wide range of challenging and problematic stress-related behaviours and formulate suitable and impactful goals.
- Put into practice their goals to manage stress and develop their personal resources for managing stress in the future.

References

Abouserie, R. (1994). Sources and levels of stress in relation to locus of control and self-esteem in university students. *Educational Psychology, 14*(3), 323–330.

Bakker, A. B., & Demerouti, E. (2016). Job demands-resources theory: Taking stock and looking forward. *Journal of Occupational Health Psychology, 22*, 273–285.

Bandura, A. (1989). Human agency in social cognitive theory. *American Psychologist, 44*(9), 1175–1184.

Burton, C. M., & King, L. A. (2009). The health benefits of writing about positive experiences: The role of broadened cognition. *Psychology & Health, 24*(8), 867–879.

Cotton, S. J., Dollard, M. F., & De Jonge, J. (2002). Stress and student job design: Satisfaction, well-being, and performance in university students. *International Journal of Stress Management, 9*(3), 147–162.

Dollard, M., Winefield, H. R., & Winefield, A. (2001). *Occupational strain and efficacy in human service workers: When the rescuer becomes the victim*. Springer Science & Business Media.

Duckworth, A. L., Peterson, C., Matthews, M. D., & Kelly, D. R. (2007). Grit: Perseverance and passion for long-term goals. *Journal of Personality and Social Psychology, 92*(6), 1087–1101.

Durand-Bush, N., McNeill, K., Harding, M., & Dobransky, J. (2015). Investigating stress, psychological well-being, mental health functioning, and self-regulation capacity among university undergraduate students: Is this population optimally functioning? *Canadian Journal of Counselling and Psychotherapy, 49*(3).

Kannangara, C. S., Allen, R. E., Waugh, G., Nahar, N., Khan, S. Z. N., Rogerson, S., & Carson, J. (2018). *All that glitters is not grit: Three studies of grit in university students* (Vol. 9, p. 1539). *Frontiers in Psychology*.

Lazarus R. S., & Folkman S. (1984). *Stress, Appraisal and Coping*. New York: Springer.

Luszczynska, A., & Schwarzer, R. (2005). The role of self-efficacy in health self-regulation. In W. Greve, K. Rothermund, & D. Wentura (Eds.), *The adaptive self: Personal continuity and intentional self-development* (pp. 137–152). Hogrefe & Huber Publishers.

Pennebaker, J. W., & Seagal, J. D. (1999). Forming a story: The health benefits of narrative. *Journal of Clinical Psychology, 55*, 1243–1254.

Pitt, A., Oprescu, F., Tapia, G., & Gray, M. (2018). An exploratory study of students' weekly stress levels and sources of stress during the semester. *Active Learning in Higher Education, 19*(1), 61–75.

Reddy K. J., Menon, K.. R., Thattil, A. (2018), Academic Stress and its Sources Among University Students. *Biomed Pharmacol Journal, 11*(1).

Schuler, R. S. (1979). Managing stress means managing time. *Personnel Journal, 58*, 851–854.

Tofi, T., Flett, R., & Timutimu-Thorpe, H. (1996). Problems faced by pacific island students at university in New Zealand: Some effects on academic performance and psychological wellbeing. *New Zealand Journal of Educational Studies, 31*(1), 51–59.

Travers, C. (2011). Unveiling a reflective diary methodology for exploring the lived experiences of stress and coping. *Journal of Vocational Behavior, 79*(1), 204–216.

Travers, C. J., & Cooper, C. L. (1991). Stress and status in teaching: An investigation of potential gender-related relationships. *Women in Management Review, 6*(4).

Travers, C. J., & Cooper, C. L. (1993). Mental health, job satisfaction and occupational stress among UK teachers. *Work & Stress, 7*(3), 203–219.

Travers, C. J., & Cooper, C. L. (1996). *Teachers under pressure. Stress in the teaching profession.* Routledge.

Webb, E., Ashton, C. H., Kelly, P., & Kamali, F. (1996). Alcohol and drug use in UK university students. *The Lancet, 348*(9032), 922–925.

CHAPTER 11

Reflective Goal Setting and Its Impact on Academic Growth and Performance

How Can Students Improve Their Academic Growth and Performance Using the Framework?

Abstract This chapter will outline how Reflective Goal Setting can be used to improve university students' academic growth and performance. Students whose experiences are detailed in this chapter had attended the semester-long module, Advanced Interpersonal Skills, outlined earlier in the book. This amounted to a fifteen week period of Reflective Goal Setting. A range of influencing factors, such as academic growth-specific goals, and key features of the model itself will be addressed. An interesting finding is that contrary to traditional Goal Setting Theory, students experience non-specific effects from general personal development goals when improving their academic performance.

Keywords Academic growth and performance • Academic goals • Growth mindsets • Non-specific effects

> "Following the Reflective Goal Setting process, I am genuinely a changed person in terms of my work ethic and ability. I can now work for hours at a time with no procrastination because I know the familiar buzz I will get when I complete the work I wanted to do."

INTRODUCTION

Though university students may have fulfilled the criteria to secure a place at university, not all students have developed the self-discipline and self-regulation strategies required for sustained independent study nor the academic abilities needed to achieve the high grades they seek in that learning context. Students may arrive at university with similar entry grades but have weaker academic skillsets to their peers. So, they may achieve varying results due to differential approaches and attitudes towards their studies (Kuh et al., 2007, 2008), or they may find it hard to keep up with the challenges of the higher education environment (Pennebaker et al., 1990).

My own observations show that despite being at university for several years, many students fall foul of their established and ineffective approaches to study in their final year. Yet, there can be a lack of support for developing their academic skills further, as tutors may assume they are fully developed by this stage. My final year students are also typically returning from an internship where their academic skills have inevitably been left to rust. In addition, higher performing students may also seek to strengthen their academic prowess further and surpass their current levels of achievement and academic growth (Dweck, 2012). So, methods for (re)developing their academic growth at this final crucial stage are especially welcome.

Reflective Goal Setting has been found to benefit students' academic growth regardless of their initial academic abilities. Various studies show that if students devote time and effort to their studies, avoid procrastination, and show persistence, they do well (Burks et al., 2015; Beattie et al., 2018; Kautz et al., 2014). This chapter will show how the model can support the development of helpful academic skillsets and mindsets.

As we saw in Chap. 3, one way to improve academic performance is via the use of positive psychology interventions, such as those employing goal setting approaches. Though such interventions in academic settings have mainly focused on younger children within a specific task or classroom context (e.g., Covington, 2000), several goal setting scholars are designing university-based programmes. For example, in addition to my own work (Travers et al., 2015), the online written narrative goal setting interventions of Morisano et al. (2010), Schippers et al. (2015), and Marschalko (2018) have all had success employing written goal setting interventions to boost students' academic performance.

The rest of this chapter will present a qualitative account of students' insights and explanations for the enhanced academic growth and increased performance they claim to experience from using Reflective Goal Setting. Students whose experiences are detailed in this chapter had attended the semester-long 'Advanced Interpersonal Skills' module outlined earlier in this book. This took part in the first semester of their final year and amounted to 15 weeks of Reflective Goal Setting on three goals of their own choosing.

How Do Students Use Reflective Goal Setting to Enhance Their Academic Growth and Performance?

Over the years of using Reflective Goal Setting with students, typically over half choose to set one or more academic growth-related goal following their self-awareness activities at Stage 1. Goals are identified once they have explored their prior experiences with academic study and attainment, gathered feedback, and explored their consistent academic story. Academic-related goals tend to fall under three themes:

- **personal organization and time management**; (e.g., *"Becoming more organised by having a timetable and to-do lists."*);
- **emotional and psychological control** (e.g., *"Not putting off the things I find most challenging."*);
- **interpersonal-skills development** (e.g., *"Being more assertive about my own opinions in group coursework meetings."*).

These academic goals are a combination of *mastery* goals (e.g., improving time management or organizational skills) and *performance* goals (e.g., obtaining a higher grade than usual). Some are related to *proximal* issues (e.g., *"To do all recommended reading as soon as I can after the lecture."*) and others to more *distal* objectives (e.g., *"To improve my final degree grade."*).

At the end of the process, using prompts, students are asked to write in-depth reflections on their experiences:

- *Do they think Reflective Goal Setting had an impact on their academic growth and performance?*
- *Have they seen any noticeable improvements in their grades?*
- *Are there any noticeable academic changes and effects related to other **non**-academic types of goals?*
- *Which key features of Reflective Goal Setting made an impact?*

What Impact Do Students Think Reflective Goal Setting Has on Their Academic Growth?

Regardless of the type of goal set, most students (over 90%), believe that academic growth has taken place because of their Reflective Goal Setting activities. At the end of the formal taught aspect of the process, these students are facing end of semester assignment deadlines and upcoming examinations, as well as preparing for the next and final semester of their studies. Access to *objective* evidence of academic growth, such as improved grades, is limited at that stage. However, several students report taking part in mid-semester assessments on their courses and have grades showing improvement—which they strongly believe is due to Reflective Goal Setting. For example, one student explains:

> "My confidence in my ability to do well has increased so much after working so hard on my goal. I got 75% in my mid-semester test, which I am certain is due to my goal effort, as I haven't had a grade like that before."

Another reports, "The only grades I have had so far are the Spanish assignments. I managed to achieve a top mark," a mark he felt sure was due to his Reflective Goal Setting activities. Others talk about anticipating academic growth due to using the model and its key features for the first time. One previously reluctant goal setter explains: "I have never before set goals in this way, preferring to just get on with work and hope for the best." They also claimed that their self-confidence was enhanced by the acquisition of Reflective Goal Setting skills and the knowledge that this could be applied more widely across their studies. Another student reports: "I have not only been on top of my work, but I have been ahead of it! My non-goal setting course mates have been begging me to tell them how I managed to do it."

Many also report that the process has enhanced their motivation and drive, which they believe will impact on their subsequent productivity and quality of their work.

What Is the Impact of Academic-Related Goals on Academic Growth?

Following Reflective Goal Setting, students can see a clear link between their academic-related goals and future performance, bolstered by their enhanced self-confidence and study ethic. Dweck (2012) might suggest this is due to the development of a 'growth mindset', essential for academic growth. For example, one goal setter explains:

> "In the past I found it too easy to doubt myself. Having goals that I have managed to stick to, has built my confidence in my ability and helped to banish the negative thoughts that often threaten to block my progress. Next semester I think I will continue to do well because I have a different mindset now."

Time management and self-organisation are popular goal topics. Following success in these areas, students report that new self-knowledge of their abilities has been gained, such as knowing that they are the kind of person who can get their work completed on time and in an effective manner. For example:

> "My academic time management goal has positively impacted on my academic growth. I have been able to keep up with lectures and revision while also working full time at my business. I hope to use Reflective Goal Setting in the future with my studies as I have seen such a positive impact and feel confident that I can apply that approach over again."

This enhances their optimism for better academic outcomes as they feel that for the first time in their academic career, their academic outcomes will match the effort they have put in. For example:

> "I set this goal specifically because I always struggle with maths... always put them off, don't spend as much time and effort on them as I should, and this is reflected in the marks that I get...However, I have been very proactive with my learning, and I am actually ahead of the targets that I set as part of my goal. As a result of this increased organisation and proactivity with the module, I am going into exam season feeling much more prepared. This gives me confidence that my mark will reflect this extra time and effort."

Students believe better academic outcomes will result from their newly developed academic self-discipline, such as keeping up with all work set each week by their lecturers. For example:

> "One clear victory for me was actually doing the article pre-read dictated by one of my courses, having actually read the relevant article before each lecture made the lecture materials more valuable and has made revision easier too."

Stage 3 of the model requires the identification of specific methods and techniques to apply to our goals. Students search for appropriate approaches to deal with the challenges of studying at this level, many of which they have never encountered before. For example, a number use the popular '*Pomodoro*' technique (Cirillo, 2006). This is a time management system that encourages users to break their available time into chunks with regular breaks. The agency to choose and then apply such techniques can result in strong psychological responses and a belief in the subsequent impact on improved academic performance. For example:

> "The Pomodoro method really worked for me. It helped me avoid procrastination and boosted my concentration. I just know it was responsible for the 70% I got on the marking assignment."

Do Non-Academic Goals Impact on Their Academic Growth?

Contrary to the major premise of Goal Setting Theory regarding task specificity, as outlined in Chap. 3, students report academic growth and performance from setting non-academic/general personal development goals. Non-specific effects result from such goals as enhanced interpersonal skills (such as avoiding phone/social media usage when with friends, assertive communication) and wellbeing and stress management (such as building resilience, improving habits such as going to the gym)

The potential detrimental effects of social media usage on students' wellbeing and performance are well-documented (Brooks, 2015; Ostic et al., 2021). So, it is no surprise that many students identify this as a goal area. They may have set a goal to reduce social media distractions to improve listening and attentiveness to others, or to reduce the harmful impact of unrealistic social comparisons on their self-esteem. However, they frequently experience benefits in their academic growth and performance as a consequence. For example:

> "Improving my communication skills by not spending as much time on my phone and allowing myself to pay more attention during personal conversations has also transferred to lectures. I now switch my phone off before entering the lecture theatre."

The impact of social media usage on students' academic performance is recognised by scholars worldwide (Zachos et al., 2018; Bernard & Dzandza, 2018; Soyemi et al., 2015). Choosing to work on social media-related goals can have far reaching benefits on desirable personal and academic outcomes.

Goals for enhancing assertiveness, for example, putting their own opinion across with friends when deciding where to go for a night out or deciding where to eat, can also have non-specific effects. For example, students report improvements in their confidence in how they approach group coursework, because of being able to clearly communicate their needs and wants:

> "I have an example which shows the impact of my general assertiveness goal, on my academic growth. I was involved in a group coursework piece which required giving a presentation, and I felt competent enough to take a leading role in the presentation and put my own ideas forward."

So, certain goals related to interpersonal skills can lead to increased individual agency and the ability to influence group learning situations to good effect.

Students also benefit from non-specific outcomes related to wellbeing goals as these can lead to increased control of their emotions and reactions—helping them academically. For example:

> "Whilst none of my goal areas have been targeted at academic growth, the fact that my well-being has increased means that I will be more capable of coping with the stress when exam time comes."

Engaging in healthy behaviours also seems to help, with one reporting that: "eating better food has also made me feel less tired and more energetic." Further, exercising and attending the gym can lead to increased self-discipline, increased energy, and greater focus and stamina when dealing with academic work. For example:

> "My studying has significantly improved as a result of the increased motivation and improvement on my well-being that the gym and improved confidence has given me. I wake up energised each morning which has helped my level of focus and attention on my work every day."

Others take part in relaxation and mindfulness techniques and find that these have a positive impact on how they deal with their work. For example:

> "Although none of my goals were on studying, distraction is a big problem for me. The meditation forces you to block out any distractions and push them away, instead focusing on the present and being aware. This has helped and I am able to do this while studying as well."

Being able to manage stress more effectively because of success with stress-related goals is also seen to positively impact on managing the pressures that come from studying at this level. For example: "Yes—I have been studying much more effectively because I have been able to reduce stress levels."

What Impact Do Features of Reflective Goal Setting Have on Academic Growth?

The model itself and the structured approach it offers equips students with a transferable framework for use in other learning scenarios, as one student explains:

> "Reflective Goal Setting taught me a framework which can be applied for any course in order to achieve good grades."

But engaging in enhanced self-awareness at Stage 1 in particular helps students get to grips with obstacles that may have hindered their previous attempts to boost their academic potential and then find ways to craft helpful and meaningful goals. As one explains:

> "Learning to love myself has also taught me to believe I deserve better and that I should want a good life for myself pushing me to want to work hard and not stay in a cycle of negative thinking towards myself."

In addition, keeping an on-going written reflective diary is especially powerful. It can encourage consistency of effort rather than last minute cramming for some. For example:

> "Knowing I need to mindfully and regularly write about my goal progress in my diary has also taught me how to concentrate on my work for longer and more consistently. My ability to focus on exam revision has increased even though none of my goals were directly related to this aspect."

The diary also helps them to manage setbacks as they occur, developing 'academic tenacity' and longer-term growth goal focus and perseverance (Dweck et al., 2011). For example:

> "I think it has allowed me to grow academically. I feel calmer and at ease with work and feel I am better equipped to handle situations that occur where, in the past, I may have got stressed. My self-efficacy has been enhanced and I have more belief in my capabilities and the choices I make. This has enabled me to think more positively about future exams and assignments and to handle them differently. I am yet to get any results back, but hopefully when I do, I will see some sort of improvement."

Research has shown that possessing good reflective-writing skills is associated with improved academic performance (Tsingos-Lucas et al., 2017). Though not all students hit the ground running with their written reflection, most develop over the duration of the process. Regular, reflective writing is viewed by some as a way of improving how they express themselves and their ideas on paper in assignments and exams. For example:

> "Keeping a regular reflective diary has certainly helped me express and structure my thoughts on complex ideas and concepts, which I am sure is standing me in good stead in my written work."

These findings suggest that Reflective Goal Setting could be implemented as a fundamental design feature in a wide variety of academic scenarios to enable students to increase their academic potential and performance, while developing their skills for employability, career success, and future leadership potential.

Summary

Reflective Goal Setting enhances students' academic growth and performance by:

- Enabling more accurate assessments of current academic abilities and attitudes to set relevant goals
- Developing self-confidence and motivation for future academic challenges,
- Learning to deal with obstacles, take responsibility for the results of their efforts, and apply learning more broadly across their studies.
- Non-specific goals impacting on attitudes and behaviours leading to academic benefits
- Developing 'academic tenacity' and 'psychological preparedness' for future academically challenging situations

References

Beattie, G., Laliberté, J. W. P., & Oreopoulos, P. (2018). Thrivers and divers: Using non-academic measures to predict college success and failure. *Economics of Education Review, 62*, 170–182.

Bernard, K. J., & Dzandza, P. E. (2018). *Effect of social media on academic performance of students in Ghanaian Universities: A case study of.* University of Ghana.

Brooks, S. (2015). Does personal social media usage affect efficiency and well-being? *Computers in Human Behavior, 46*, 26–37.

Burks, S. V., Lewis, C., Kivi, P. A., Wiener, A., Anderson, J. E., Götte, L., DeYoung, C. G., & Rustichini, A. (2015). Cognitive skills, personality, and economic preferences in collegiate success. *Journal of Economic Behavior & Organization, 115*, 30–44.

Cirillo, F. (2006). The pomodoro technique (the pomodoro). *Agile Processes in Software Engineering, 54*(2), 35.

Covington, M. V. (2000). Goal theory, motivation, and school achievement: An integrative review. *Annual Review of Psychology, 51*(1), 171–200.

Dweck, C. S. (2012). Mindsets and human nature: Promoting change in the Middle East, the schoolyard, the racial divide, and willpower. *American Psychologist, 67*(8), 614.

Dweck, C., Walton, G., M., & Cohen, G., L. (2011). *Academic tenacity: Mindsets and skills that promote long-term learning.* Seattle, WA: Gates Foundation.

Kautz, T., Heckman, J. J., Diris, R., Ter Weel, B., & Borghans, L. (2014). *Fostering and measuring skills: Improving cognitive and non-cognitive skills to promote lifetime success.* Working Paper 20749. National Bureau of Economic Research. http://www.nber.org/papers/w20749

Kuh, G., D., Kinzie, J., Buckley, J., A., Bridges, B., K., & Hayek, J., C. (2007). Piecing Together the Student Success Puzzle: Research, Propositions, and Recommendations. *ASHE Higher Education Report, 32*(5). San Francisco: Jossey-Bass.

Kuh, G. D., Cruce, T. M., Shoup, R., Kinzie, J., & Gonyea, R. M. (2008). Unmasking the effects of student engagement on first-year college grades and persistence. *The Journal of Higher Education, 79*(5), 540–563.

Marschalko, E. E., Morisano, D., & Szamoskozi, I. (2018). Goal-setting among STEM and non-STEM students: A pilot randomised controlled trial. In E. Locke & M. Schippers (Eds.), *Improving lives: Personal goal setting boosts student performance and happiness.* Academy of Management Annual Meeting Proceedings: 2018:1, https://doi.org/10.5465/AMBPP.2018.16790 symposium

Morisano, D., Hirsh, J. B., Peterson, J. B., Pihl, R. O., & Shore, B. M. (2010). Setting, elaborating, and reflecting on personal goals improves academic performance. *Journal of Applied Psychology, 95*(2), 255.

Ostic, D., Qalati, S. A., Barbosa, B., Shah, S. M. M., Galvan Vela, E., Herzallah, A. M., & Liu, F. (2021). Effects of social media use on psychological well-being: A mediated model. *Frontiers in Psychology, 12*, 2381.

Pennebaker, J. W., Colder, M., & Sharp, L. K. (1990). Accelerating the coping process. *Journal of Personality and Social Psychology, 58*(3), 528.

Schippers, M. C., Scheepers, A. W., & Peterson, J. B. (2015). A scalable goal-setting intervention closes both the gender and ethnic minority achievement gap. *Palgrave Communications, 1*(1), 1–12.

Soyemi, J., Oloruntoba, S. A., & Okafor, B. (2015). Analysis of mobile phone impact on student academic performance in tertiary institution. *International Journal of Emerging Technology and Advanced Engineering, 5*(1), 361–365.

Travers, C. J., Morisano, D., & Locke, E. A. (2015). Self-reflection, growth goals, and academic outcomes: A qualitative study. *British Journal of Educational Psychology, 85*(2), 224–241.

Tsingos-Lucas, C., Bosnic-Anticevich, S., Schneider, C. R., & Smith, L. (2017). Using reflective writing as a predictor of academic success in different assessment formats. *American Journal of Pharmaceutical Education, 81*(1).

Zachos, G., Paraskevopoulou-Kollia, E. A., & Anagnostopoulos, I. (2018). Social media use in higher education: A review. *Education Sciences, 8*(4), 194.

CHAPTER 12

Reflective Goal Setting for Leader Personal Development

How Can We Use the Model to Develop Crucial Leader Skills?

Abstract This chapter will share insights from three case organisations who sought to enhance the personal development of their managers and leaders. Using Reflective Goal Setting, a range of crucial leader skills were targeted within a range of organisational contexts. Focusing on a selection of experiences, the chapter identifies how the key features of Reflective Goal Setting enabled the identification and implementation of challenging goals to improve leader behaviour and impact. Reflective Goal Setting improved the delivery of services in a health care setting, the development of more effective performance management in a finance organisation, and the enhancement of team leadership in an agroscience company.

Keywords Leader personal development • Authentic Leadership • Leader self-awareness

© The Author(s), under exclusive license to Springer Nature Switzerland AG 2022
C. J. Travers, *Reflective Goal Setting*,
https://doi.org/10.1007/978-3-030-99228-6_12

Introduction

> **Hardwiring of Leader Goals in AgroSci**
> "I have always been a bit of a 'reflector', but Reflective Goal Setting has taught me about taking control and responsibility, being proactive, having a sense of purpose, understanding self and others, and focussing on what is important. Also, being the 'best self' I can be in service to those I lead, and for the successful achievement of their goals. I can attest to the benefit of writing within the framework, as it 'hardwired' my goals into actual behaviour. Stopping to ponder and reflect organised my thoughts and lead to renewed energy and achievement resulting in a spiral culminating in a pleasant feeling of greater sense of self-efficacy."—Leader at AgroSci
>
> "The single biggest way to impact an organization is to focus on leadership development. There is almost no limit to the potential of an organization that recruits good people, raises them up as leaders and continually develops them."—John Maxwell

Over the last 30 years, I have worked with many managers and leaders across a variety of organisational settings, in private, public and voluntary sectors—such as engineering; finance, construction, medicine and health, health and social care, travel and adventure, sports, and recreation, agroscience, and automotive. A great number have been participants on bespoke master's programmes designed and delivered by myself and my colleagues at Loughborough University School of Business and Economics. Others have been delegates on tailored non-accredited courses or known to me in a consultant capacity. One of the most pleasing aspects of this work is that regardless of the sector they work in, or the level achieved in their career, they have a common need and drive to develop their leadership skills. Naturally, skills required will vary with education, job status, and experience, but most are able to identify challenging and worthwhile goal areas to work on. Interestingly, many of those leaders still find elusive many of those same skills my final year students seek to improve.

Leaders' soft skills are increasingly in demand due to the impact they can have on organisational success and employee performance, motivation, and wellbeing (AbuJbara & Worley, 2018). Leadership has always been difficult during challenging times, but the unique stressors facing organisations in contemporary organisations, whatever sector, require leader self-awareness, purpose, values, and integrity. Many theories of leadership are on offer to explain how to develop leaders; however, my preferred approach is to explore and apply the concept of 'authentic leadership.' According to authentic leadership theory, leaders can be considered authentic when they (a) know who they are and (b) consistently enact their values and beliefs (Gardner et al., 2011). Defined in various ways, the essence of authentic leadership is "being true to one's self" (George & Sims, 2007; Ilies et al., 2005). As a concept, it is not without its critics, but there are several helpful components which feature in most theories outlining authentic leadership, one being self-awareness—a key feature of Reflective Goal Setting.

Some argue that it is a leader's moral duty to personally develop, for example, developing their identity and moral leadership (Caldwell, 2012), self-efficacy and self-concept (Smith & Woodworth, 2012), and self-awareness and emotional intelligence (Showry & Manasa, 2014). As leaders work on their self-awareness and strive to achieve excellence, they may recognise that developing their skills enables them to unlock the potential of their organisations and those with whom they work (Chatterjee, 1998). Theory and evidence surrounding authentic leadership shows that authenticity can influence a range of positive outcomes among followers, leaders, groups, and organisations (Gardner et al., 2011). For example, improved organisational and follower performance (Hmieleski et al., 2012; Leroy et al., 2015), lower employee burnout (Laschinger & Fida, 2014), and higher work engagement and job satisfaction (Giallonardo et al., 2010). Reflective Goal Setting aims to work on the development of leader authenticity by helping leaders gain greater self-insight to set more personally relevant and impactful goals. As Goffee and Jones would advise, "be yourself but with more skill!" (2015).

To develop authentic leadership, we need to devise processes that can be utilised in an on-going way and where leaders gain self-awareness enabling them to establish relationships with their employees which are open, transparent, and genuine. Development of these skills cannot be achieved with a quick fix. Leader development is inherently longitudinal (Day, 2011) involving a process by which leaders acquire relevant experiences, skills, behaviours, and knowledge over time (Lord & Hall, 2005).

Research demonstrates the value and benefits of interventions in developing leaders (Avolio et al., 2009), though little insight is offered into the longitudinal processes of leader development (Day & Dragoni, 2015). Leaders need the opportunities to practise leadership skills that will strengthen their self-perception as a leader and therefore motivate leader identity change. Reflective Goal Setting is an attempt to encourage leaders to engage in on-going personal, goal supported development.

As we discussed in Chap. 3, traditional goal setting approaches can have limited effectiveness in the development of 'softer' yet crucial leadership skills. Perhaps this is due to a lack of self-awareness and how to turn self-insight gains into powerful and sustainable goals and actions. Several leader Reflective Goal Setting experiences have been shared elsewhere throughout the book, but here I will briefly showcase a few case examples to highlight the wider impact of the goals beyond the individual leaders themselves. Much of the impact of soft skills development is hard to measure in quantitative terms. But some of these examples can demonstrate the more objective impact.

How Can Reflective Goal Setting Be Used to Improve Leader Personal Development?

The following cases are used to illustrate the varied impact of Reflective Goal Setting when used by leaders from three client organisations with whom I have worked in recent years.

Case Example 1: Improved Safety and Patient Care at NorthHosp NHS Trust

NorthHosp is one of the UK's largest and busiest acute hospital trusts, employing almost 20,000 staff over several hospitals. They were seeking to develop a highly engaged, high performing workforce, and a patient-centred culture through empowerment in all sections and levels. The business manager of their Organisational Learning Department approached the Executive Education team in my Business School and asked us to share our expertise as part of their staff professional development programme. Following an analysis of training and development needs, we designed and delivered a Leadership in Healthcare course attended by medical and operational staff in management and leadership roles. Covering subjects such as the leadership context, team working, leadership style, self-awareness, their learning was underpinned by Reflective Goal Setting. They were assessed by a piece of work requiring them to identify and implement a personal leadership development goal using Reflective Goal Setting and to diarise their attempts. Participants identified a range of suitable skills to work on including: developing impactful presentations; improving communication in meetings; improving emotional self-control in interactions with colleagues; developing active listening to prevent interrupting others when they are speaking; gaining confidence to develop professionalism in a new leadership role; enhancing ability and willingness to lead at an operational level; developing more effective delegation strategies; developing a situational approach to leading team members; being able to give constructive feedback to team members when service expectations are not being met.

Following taught sessions which covered Reflective Goal Setting and theories and frameworks related to leader goal areas, they returned to the workplace to put those goals into practice and then reported back on their progress and impact. In many cases, their claims for impact were corroborated by their own line managers in follow up interviews. What follows are three illustrations which showcase the use and impact of the model in practice and developments deemed as especially powerful by the senior leaders sponsoring the programme.

Increasing Asbestos Safety
Using Reflective Goal Setting, one leader was able to complete the specification of a new asbestos management contract which incorporated new mechanisms of control, improving on the ad-hoc reactive element previously employed. The new contract featured a built-in process, compliant with legislation, that provided non-specialists with the steps to follow when asbestos surveys were required. This allowed project and estate staff to self-manage this aspect of asbestos control. Previously, this leader would have had to be involved on an almost constant basis which was a source of great frustration. Reflective Goal Setting enabled her to achieve a process that would free up capacity and allow managers to help themselves in this specialist area. Use of the model also helped her create the supporting work environment in which this new approach would be successful. As a result of working on her delegation skills, she reported, "Engaging others with what I do and giving them ownership of the delegated tasks and responsibilities has resulted in greater understanding for them and some assistance for me, which in turn, streamlines what we do."

Her line manager also reported a visible change in her working practices which highlighted her use of the model, that is, taking a new approach to work; delegation of tasks to others; taking a step-back and growing in confidence; implementation of a new policy in their area; seeing the need to develop the skills of others to help them achieve their work objectives, deal with cost-cutting and limited resources and put appropriate training in place; identify their own training needs and longer-term career goals. Others in the organisation also commented on the change they had seen in this leader personally and professionally, especially in the way she now opened up to others on a more personal level.

She reported feeling hopeful for future application of her new skills: "I am hoping to be able to pass on part of my work to a group of people who will be trained, have each other to help and me to fall back on and mentor them where needed. This will enable me to progress to other things and hopefully move on their careers too, in turn improving the organisation."

Improving a Junior Doctor Support Service
Another attendee of this programme used Reflective Goal Setting in the successful introduction of a change in service provision for junior doctors to access deteriorating patients. She reported: "I have introduced 24/7 working and 12-hour shift pattern successfully, with team member satisfaction, in a team that was initially extremely resistant to change. The team have since become more accepting of change in general and are supportive of planned changes on the horizon." Where everyone typically saw problems and issues rather than solutions, she used Reflective Goal Setting principles to help her adapt her leadership style to be more participatory with her team to achieve consensus on goals and to overcome barriers in her team. She reported that the Reflective Goal Setting process was really useful for this particular aspect of her role and affirmed that its features definitely helped with buy-in; without which she felt resistance would have been longer lasting and its implementation delayed. Her support had been positively received by the Trust and resulted in a 33% reduction in cardio arrest calls. She now plans to introduce a new patient-centred and cost-effective rehabilitation service aligned to various stakeholders' strategy. In addition, her line manager has seen a change in her approach since using Reflective Goal Setting including more trust in and empowerment of others, more engagement with and listening to others, and an overall growth in her confidence.

Improving a Medical Equipment Safety Protocol
This leader, based in Clinical Engineering Services used Reflective Goal Setting to work on developing a range of leadership communication approaches that could be matched to the situation and achieved

changes concerning the safety of medical equipment within the department. As a result, these changes are sustainable as they have led to important cultural changes and staff members are now more responsive to dealing with medical equipment safety. They also used the principles of the model to task others and establish an agreement to work in more efficient ways, and further plans have been made to use the approach to set up a new service within the organisation. She reflects and comments: "I found the Reflective Goal-Setting process effective at developing my learning... I'm now more aware that I can support others to take on tasks and be accountable for work, and then I can learn from that interaction. I have practiced a range of communication styles to support that approach."

Since she embarked on using Reflective Goal Setting, their line manager noticed a change in her leadership style from autocratic to collaborative saying: "She listens to others more and adjusts her position accordingly." She is now more focused on the department and the end goal, rather than being just performance driven. Her line manager believes that part of the success may be down to the environment created by the Trust Chief Executive who is supportive of the Reflective Goal Setting approach and instigated the leader development programme in the first place.

Case 2: Improving Performance Management Among MutualAssoc Members

MutualAssoc represents UK building societies and credit unions and their 43,000 full and part-time staff across approximately 1380 branches. Their senior leadership approached my Executive Education Team to create a bespoke MSc in Strategic Leadership for Financial Mutuals. They had identified a need to develop a new generation of talented leaders growing through the organisation and wider financial mutual sector with a deep understanding of mutual and co-operative businesses. The programme was launched at their 2015 annual conference where I presented a keynote address outlining the potential for Reflective Goal Setting. This was primarily to achieve buy-in from senior leaders by promoting a key feature of the upcoming programme, that is, the development of leaders' soft and interpersonal skills to enhance motivational and inspirational leadership in their member organisations. Once on the programme, delegates covered many subjects including leadership theory, team working, marketing, finance, etc. They were asked to set personal development goals at the start of the programme and for each new module using Reflective Goal Setting. This was accompanied by an on-going reflective diary of their goal setting attempts and progress. They presented posters to key leaders in the business at special events and submitted portfolios detailing their development journeys and goal progress. Two cases were highlighted by their CEO as especially demonstrating the positive impact that Reflective Goal Setting had on the business.

Development of a New Appraisal Framework
Following Reflective Goal Setting, one leader set a goal to critique and implement change within the performance appraisal process in their Credit Union. The resulting new appraisal process is now focussed on personal growth and development, which was a key area of the plan they were attempting to develop. They report that each member of their team is now able to set their own goals and work with the team leader towards meeting them. They are also working continually to increase knowledge of the business, enabling each member to understand their place in the strategic plan. Previously, they had observed that there was disparity in the use of appraisal documents across the business. Corroborating the leaders' claims for impact, MutualAssoc's CEO says: "Using the Reflective Goal Setting principles as taught on the programme has been fundamental in their development of a standardised process that enables managers to appraise individuals more effectively. Importantly, the model has also helped the development of the presentation and communication skills necessary to support take-up of the improved approach."

Improving the Delivery of 'Balanced' Feedback for Improved Performance Management
Another leader on the programme used their Reflective Goal Setting training to set a goal to improve how they used feedback as an aspect of their leadership. They identified that they previously felt reluctant to give both positive and negative feedback to reports and would especially avoid the more critical and negative. Reflective Goal Setting principles helped them communicate developmental aspects with their team and they were also able to share this new learning with another colleague. Among other benefits, several months on they reflected that: "I now (unless absolutely necessary) do not reschedule performance review meetings—I understand the significance of these reviews and appreciate the negative impact on team members should these need to be rearranged." and further, "I invest more time in the preparatory work. So, I am prepared and briefed on activity undertaken." Surprisingly, they also reported: "I have no hesitation now

in discussing sensitive matters. I position aspects that require discussion, which are negative or are development areas in a constructive way." Reflective Goal Setting has been fundamental in this leader's personal development and their approach to providing developmental feedback to others in their team.

Case 3: Improving Team Performance at AgroSci

AgroSci is an international group of laboratories, providing testing and support services to the pharmaceutical, food, environmental, agroscience, and consumer products industries and to governments. They have over 50,000 staff across a network of more than 900 independent companies in over 50 countries and operate more than 800 laboratories. AgroSci offers a portfolio of over 200,000 analytical methods for evaluating the safety, identity, composition, authenticity, origin, and purity of biological substances and products, and also for innovative clinical diagnostics.

Since 2018, the Executive Education team of my business school has run two leadership programmes for AgroSci. A need was identified to enhance the goal setting skills and resilience of the business's upcoming leaders. I and my colleagues worked with their Human Resources Director, responsible for all HR and personal development activities across their business, to design and develop relevant programmes, and have so far delivered training for two cohorts, plus senior leaders from across Europe and the US. This has included material on becoming a more resilient leader, where leaders were introduced to Reflective Goal Setting to aid the successful transfer of learning from the programme and to gain crucial leader self-insight, interpersonal skills, and develop specific knowledge. The benefits have been far reaching for the leaders themselves, their teams, and the wider organisation. Leaders were invited to set personal development goals at the start of the programme, document goal attempts, and explore goal progress in follow-up group sessions and some interviews. Reflective Goal Setting is on-going, but two examples demonstrate the positive impact that use of the model has had on these leaders.

Reducing Task Backlog and Improving Turnaround in the Quality Assurance (QA) Team

This leader's role was involved in quality assurance and they held responsibility for regulatory compliance across eight different sites in the USA. He used the model to tackle a deteriorating situation at one of the large residue chemistry sites, where work was piling up and morale was low. Using the process, he reorganised the leadership and appointed one manager over all service line quality assurance units. At the time these changes were introduced (May 2020), there were 90 active tasks on record, which accounted for a 12-week backlog if the Quality Assurance team ignored all other incoming work, so effectively a 6-month backlog. In addition, there were approximately 15 internal audits to complete, that formed part of a regulatory requirement.

He reports: "As of late December 2020, there were no active tasks on record, and all internal audit tasks had been completed. Where previously QA tasks would be generated with a 2-week turnaround, they are now being turned within 3-5 days." He reports that Reflective Goal Setting was fundamental to the success of this process, partly because it helped him re-evaluate what had been his home site from a more corporate perspective. "Through hard work and some difficult changes, the differences between pre and post goals are like night and day." "As I look to the future, I am convinced that Reflective Goal Setting will be an important part of my management toolkit."

Improving Sales Figures and Team Functioning
This leader is a key accounts manager in the USA. She was struggling to keep up with her workload and feeling overwhelmed. She reports: "Prior to adopting Reflective Goal Setting I was feeling overwhelmed with the sheer volume of work and had been reluctant to delegate, always preferring to complete the required work and avoid the time-costly explanations and questions that inevitably follow. So, my approach has historically been to take on more and more work until 'something gives'. Using self-reflection, I recognised that delegation was a fundamental element of my leadership role." Using Reflective Goal Setting, she set her goal around delegation with a view to developing her team and reducing her personal workload. Her actions: "I initially offered up easier duties to my team, progressing to bigger and more complex tasks as their skills developed and my confidence in their capability grew." These aims have been achieved. For example, her team members are observably engaging in more independent problem-solving. Also, she achieved around 115% of her annual sales target (Target $21.27 m vs $24.3 m sales) even before year end. Before using the features of the model, she had never reached 100% of the sales target in the type of role she currently occupies. She says: "I am in no doubt that Reflective Goal Setting was fundamental in achieving these

increases in performance and management design changes. Looking forward to 2021, I intend to use Reflective Goal Setting more widely in exploiting new business potential and aligning business strategy across the organisation."

Summary

Using Reflective Goal Setting, managers and leaders can:

- Successfully transfer their learning from leadership development programmes back into their workplace.
- Develop skills across a range of areas that not only benefit them individually, but their teams and organisations.
- Enhance their leader self-confidence and self-efficacy.
- Impact on a variety of leader challenges across their businesses.

References

AbuJbara, N. A. K., & Worley, J. A. (2018). Leading toward new horizons with soft skills. *On The Horizon-The Strategic Planning Resource for Education Professionals, 26*(3), 247–259.

Avolio, B. J., Walumbwa, F. O., Weber, T. J., (2009). Leadership: Current Theories, Research, and Future Directions, *Annual Review of Psychology, 60*(1), 421–449.

Caldwell, C. (2012). *Moral leadership: A transformative model for tomorrow's leaders.* Business Expert Press.

Chatterjee, D. (1998). *Leading consciously: A pilgrimage toward self-mastery.* Butterworth-Heinemann.

Day, D. V. (2011). Leadership development. *The SAGE Handbook of Leadership, 22*, 37–50.

Day, D. V., & Dragoni, L. (2015). Leadership development: An outcome-oriented review based on time and levels of analyses. *Annual Review of Organizational Psychology and Organizational Behavior, 2*(1), 133–156.

Gardner, W. L., Cogliser, C. C., Davis, K. M., & Dickens, M. P. (2011). Authentic leadership: A review of the literature and research agenda. *The Leadership Quarterly, 22*(6), 1120–1145.

George, W., & Sim, P. (2007). *True north: Discover your authentic leadership.* Jossey-Bass.

Giallonardo, L. M., Wong, C. A., & Iwasiw, C. L. (2010). Authentic leadership of preceptors: Predictor of new graduate nurses' work engagement and job satisfaction. *Journal of Nursing Management, 18*(8), 993–1003.

Goffee, R., & Jones, G. (2015). *Why should anyone be led by You? With a new preface by the Authors: What it takes to be an authentic leader.* Harvard Business Review Press.

Hmieleski, H., Cole, M. S., & Baron, R. A. (2012). Shared authentic leadership and new venture performance. *Journal of Management, 38*(5), 1476–1499.

Ilies, R., Morgeson, F. P., & Nahrgang, J. D. (2005). Authentic leadership and eudaemonic well-being: Understanding leader–follower outcomes. *The Leadership Quarterly, 16*(3), 373–394.

Laschinger, H. K. S., & Fida, R. (2014). New nurses, burnout and workplace wellbeing: The influence of authentic leadership and psychological capital. *Burnout Research, 1*(1), 19–28.

Leroy, H., Anseel, F., Gardner, W. L., & Sels, L. (2015). Authentic leadership, authentic followership, basic need satisfaction, and work role performance a cross-level study. *Journal of Management, 41*(6), 1677–1697.

Lord, R. G., & Hall, R. J. (2005). Identity, deep structure and the development of leadership skill. *The Leadership Quarterly, 16*(4), 591–615.

Showry, M., & Manasa, K. V. L. (2014). Self-awareness-key to effective leadership. *IUP Journal of Soft Skills, 8*(1).

Smith, I. H., & Woodworth, W. P. (2012). Developing social entrepreneurs and social innovators: A social identity and self-efficacy approach. *Academy of Management Learning & Education, 11*(3), 390–407.

CHAPTER 13

Conclusions

Where Can We Take Reflective Goal Setting From Here?

Abstract In Part I, we explored the theoretical foundations of Reflective Goal Setting, then, in Part II, we learnt how to use it—stage by stage. Finally, in Part III, we examined some examples of its impact on specific goal areas in varying contexts. The model is not exclusive to those settings and skills however, so this final chapter will conclude with suggestions of where Reflective Goal Setting could also make an impact: that is, learning, teaching, leading, researching, and coaching.

Keywords Coaching · Personal development · Grow model · Research

Introduction

We have seen that Reflective Goal Setting builds on classic theoretical approaches to goal setting by placing a major emphasis on self-awareness, visualization, writing about goals in detail, and on-going written reflection in the pursuit of improved personal development and the acquisition of soft skills. It also challenges a key feature of Goal Setting Theory; that of specificity. Setting goals in one area can benefit us in other domains. An example being academic growth, as seen in Chap. 11.

The model should be viewed as an on-going cyclical process, and something we can either use continuously to develop, or return to at times when we need to develop new skills or ratchet up those we already have. The model can develop our self-efficacy regarding our current and future goal setting.

We have seen its versatility with a range of skills hitherto considered hard to operationalise and measure—it can toughen up our soft skills for success. What started out as a framework for aiding interpersonal skills development can be applied to life skills in general via its active ingredients, especially the power of on-going written reflection.

The model shows us that we can engage in personal development at any time and in any scenario, especially when engaging in new or existing leadership roles. Not everyone has the luxury of being mentored or coached in their organisation or provided with soft skills development during their university course. So, it is proposed as a means of 'self-coaching,' though it can clearly be used for coaching others.

Authenticity is key, in the sense that we can explore who we are, then build on that. It is not about changing who you are but being a more skilled version of yourself.

> **Goals.** "There's no telling what you can do when you get inspired by them. There's no telling what you can do when you believe in them. And there's no telling what will happen when you act upon them."—Jim Rohn

I Am a Student: How Can I Use Reflective Goal Setting?

Many of the illustrations outlined in this book are derived from the experiences of final year business and management students. But the framework can be used to enhance *any* learning experience in *any* educational setting. You may well be studying engineering, software design, or English literature, but the desire for personal development in such areas as: academic growth, management of stress and coping, relationships and interactions with others, employability and professionalism, and skills for future leadership are essentially the same.

Many university and college departments choose not to focus on these skills in their curriculum or provide opportunities to develop them, therefore it is even more important to find ways to work on them for yourself. The student journey has many key transitional stages: arriving at university from school or college, moving into a new year group, securing, and working in job internships, moving out into the world of work following graduation. Each transition requires the development of different and additional skills and mindsets. You may need to create a better impression at interview, perform better in an internship, motivate yourself to study, cope with the stress of learning at a high level, improve your relationships, enhance your academic growth, etc. Mapping your goals alongside your values at each stage, is a great way to support your distal goals of employability and career success.

I Am a University Teacher: How Can I Support My Students by Using the Model?

The pastoral role of a personal tutor is increasingly demanding. Students present with many different needs for support and development based on the challenging experiences in higher educational settings. Reflective Goal Setting can provide a structure for productive goal-based conversations with students at various stages of their university life. For example, during the transition to university, job search, adapting to placements, studying for final exams, dealing with changes in their personal lives. It can also help us write more appropriate and fitting references for those students—references that indicate we know something about them, their motivations, skill sets, and career goals.

Reflective Goal Setting can also be used as the transfer of learning tool for any module we design and deliver. We may position Reflective Goal Setting as a capstone module to support development across a range of modules or study year. As part of that, students are not only expected to develop knowledge of the specific topic area content, but also to set related personal development goals linked to the topic. For example, they might be studying a finance module and find it doesn't suit them and so struggle with the content. They could set a goal on familiarising themselves with financial documents and reading the financial pages of a newspaper to develop confidence and increase knowledge within the field. Many students struggle with topics because they lack self-awareness around their own barriers and affective responses to the topic area. Reflective Goal Setting can help them gain relevant self-insight to reduce these barriers and aid their learning.

I Am a Researcher: How Can I Use It?

Reflective Goal Setting has become my primary research area, but it could be used by fellow researchers to explore transfer of learning, personal development, and soft skills acquisition across a range of occupations, and work settings. For example, I recently became aware of a researcher utilising the model successfully with software developers (Meyer et al., 2019).

It's a great opportunity to gather data on peoples' learning and development, especially via the use of on-going written reflection. More objective measures of the impact could also be gathered; an area I am investigating currently. The approach allows us to explore the 'black box' of the goal setting process and identify the active ingredients to enable more effective future interventions.

I Am a Leader: How Can I Use It?

Reflective Goal Setting can be used for your own personal development, as seen throughout the book. It can also be used within our teams. For example, we can apply the stages of the model at the group/team level: Stage 1: Enhancing team-awareness, Stage 2: Selecting suitable team goals; Stage 3: Visualising successful team behaviours; Stage 4: Formulating a team goal; and Stage 5: Putting it into practice as a team. The team can regularly document progress and collectively reflect and review. Team members can set their own reflective goals to be compatible with that of the overall team. From my experience of working with teams, they rarely prioritise making time to stop and review how things are going. The framework offers a structure for on-going review and feedback.

On-going Reflective Goal Setting can also support regular performance management discussions. As opposed to the less effective yearly appraisal, conversations can be more fluid and goal focussed using a common goal development language.

I Am a Coach: How Can I Use It?

Reflective Goal Setting can also be used to support coaching conversations and transfer goals from coaching sessions back into the workplace. There are several popular coaching models around, the most popular of which is probably Whitmore's 'Grow' Model (2002). But Reflective Goal Setting works with soft skills and the on-going reflection gives more structure with which to support our coaching. Coachees can also have greater independence between sessions due to having an interim process to follow and feed back on at the next coaching encounter.

One idea would be to explore the potential for using AI to provide Reflective Goal Setting in coaching. For example, could a chatbot support a client in between sessions by asking the right questions and offering reflective prompts? This is not suggesting AI replace the coach, but I'm sure there's a halfway house where AI-generated suggestions could augment the coaching experience.

SO, OVER TO YOU!

There will be other ways and contexts where Reflective Goal Setting can make a contribution and it would be great to hear from you about them. Maybe you could take another look at the checklist in Appendix 1 now, and see if you can add in more ticks! In the meantime, I will leave you with one recent piece of unsolicited feedback from a final year university student as I was putting the finishing touches to this book.

> "I am just e-mailing to say thank-you because without you and your module's help, I would never have landed a job in Madrid!
> Working towards my goals allowed me to push myself and take a gap year rather than going straight into a boring grad job. I found out this morning that I got offered the job I applied for in Madrid and will be moving in November (by myself & I don't even know Spanish!). I can't believe the effect the module has had on me and my future and just wanted to say a huge THANKYOU!!!!!"

REFERENCES

Meyer, A. N., Murphy, G. C., Zimmermann, T., & Fritz, T. (2019). Enabling good work habits in software developers through reflective goal-setting. *IEEE Transactions on Software Engineering, 47*(9), 1872–1885.

Whitmore, J. (2002). *Coaching for performance: Growing people, performance and purpose* (3rd ed.). Nicholas Brealey Publishing.

Index

A
Abstract conceptualization, 53
Academic abilities, 7, 154, 163
Academically struggling, 42
Academic goals, 43, 155, 159–161
Academic growth and performance, 41, 153, 155, 159, 163
Academic tenacity, 162, 163
Accountability, 101, 113, 150
Active ingredients, 81, 101, 122, 130, 134, 148, 178, 180
Active listening, 102, 126
Adaptability, 24, 90
Adult learning, 25–27
Adult learning theory, 25, 27
Adult well-being, 76
Aggressive behaviour, 89
AI, 181
Ajzen's Theory of Planned Behaviour, 101
Alcohol consumption and drug taking, 142
Andragogy, 25, 26
Annual sales target, 174

Anxiety, 70, 91, 114, 135, 141, 142, 144, 145, 147
Appraisal, 4, 73, 74, 142, 172, 180
Appraisal Theory, 140
Arrogance, 94
Assertive, 12–13, 40, 80, 89, 116, 155, 159
Assertiveness, 85, 89, 104, 114, 118, 121, 159, 160
Assessment centres, 86
Authentic, 9, 58, 79, 80, 167
Authenticity, 9, 14, 59, 67, 167, 178
Autocratic leadership style, 171
Automatic thoughts, 36

B
Backstage self, 129
Bakker, A. B., 141
Bandura, 40, 69, 141
Behavioural intentions, 38
Behaviour change, ix, 15, 22, 39, 44
Being held accountable, 128
Berne's Transactional Analysis, 116

Bespoke master's programmes, 166
Best practise, 5, 14, 102, 115
Black box, 39, 180
Blind-self, 71
Body image, 131
Body language, 11, 108, 115
Brainstorm, 14
Breathing techniques, 100, 135
Business and management education, 15, 23, 27
Business schools, ix, 23
Business value measures, 28

C
Calibrate, 9, 118
Calibration, 14
Careers, 24
Career stages, 24
Carnegie, Dale, 10
Charisma, 50
Childhood characteristics, 76
Coaching, vii, x, 14, 25, 28, 37, 59, 178, 180, 181
Cognitive processing, 26, 43
Collaborative leadership style, 171
Collectivistic culture, 79
Communication, x, 6, 10–12, 16, 69, 86, 95, 159, 169, 171, 172
Complex motor skills, 99
Concrete as opposed to abstract goals, 43
Conscious goals, 35
Consistent story, 4, 14, 76–78, 88
Contemporary organisations, 167
Coping skills, 140
Core values, 9
Covey, Steven, 68
Cranfield, Jack, 98
Critically reflect, 59
Critical thinking, 24

Csikszentmihalyi, M., 106
Curriculum, 7, 23, 29, 178
Cyclical process, 177

D
Dark side of reflective practise, 52
Deci, E. L., 41
Decision-making, 49, 52, 69, 122
Deeply rooted aspects, 148
Degree of difficulty, 40
Delegate, 22, 26, 66, 174
Delegation, 22, 26, 104, 169, 170, 174
Demerouti, E., 141
Depression, 69, 70, 141
Detailed goal statement, 6, 39, 43, 114, 117, 120–123, 143, 146–148
Dewey, 49, 50, 54
Diary, xix, 6, 15, 34, 40, 47–60, 85, 88, 95, 117, 130–135, 140, 144, 148–150, 161, 162, 171
Diary writing skills, 59–60
Dissonance, 52, 133
Distal goals, 41, 42, 119, 128, 155, 179
Do your best goals, 38, 114
Dunning-Kruger effect, 72

E
Early adulthood, 24
Embodying a skill, 53
Emerging adulthood, 24
Emotional and psychological control, 155
Emotional reactions, 37, 50
Emotions, role of in reflection, 50
Empathic listening, 102, 126
Empathising, 11
Empathy, 70, 91, 102, 122

Employability, ix, 6, 7, 15, 100, 162, 178, 179
Enhancing self-awareness, 4, 142–144
Eureka moment, 9, 135, 149
Eurich, T., 68, 70
Evaluating, 5, 27–29
Evaluation, 25, 27–29, 49, 54, 77, 146
Evaluative framework, 29
Evidence-based action, 149
Evidence-based solutions, 11
Exam stress, 147
Executive education, 28
Executives, 7
Exercise, 26, 69, 70, 88, 133, 140
Exposure therapy, 100
External self-awareness, 70
Extrovert, 91
Extroverted behaviour, 13

F
Feedback, xiv, 4, 7, 12–14, 23, 34, 36, 38, 40, 41, 71, 73–75, 89, 90, 93–95, 102, 107–108, 112, 114, 118, 121, 122, 126, 131, 140, 145, 146, 148, 155, 169, 172–173, 180
Festinger, Leon, 70
Final year of university, 49, 127, 139
Fitness goals, 34, 49, 80, 113, 129, 131, 132
Flexibility, 24, 90, 145
Flourishing, 131
Flow, 106
Folkman, Susan, 140
Formulating a goal statement, 5, 111–123
Freud, Sigmund, 101

G
General population, 141
Gibbs' Reflective Cycle, 54
Goal committment, 38, 41, 56, 57, 119
Goal congruence with self, 41
Goal definition, x, xiii, xv, 4–6, 10–15, 29, 34–44, 48–51, 53–60, 67, 69, 71, 72, 74–76, 79, 81, 87–92, 94–97, 100–103, 105–108, 111–113, 117, 118, 120–122, 127, 128, 131–135, 139, 140, 143–150, 153, 156–162, 168, 169, 171, 174, 179, 180
Goal formulation, 49, 114, 127
Goal ideation, viii, 49, 113
Goal implementation, viii, 25, 39, 43, 49, 113, 170
Goal propensity, 128, 142
Goal Setting Theory, 12, 33–44, 89, 177
Goal specificity, 40
Goal strategies, ix, 9, 43, 103, 130, 140–142, 145, 147, 149, 150, 154, 169
Goffman, E., 129
Good practise, 102–103
Grit, 142
Group presentation, 100
Group situations, 85
Groupthink, 92

H
Habit, 36
Handwritten reflections and diaries, 57
Happiness, ix, 35, 41, 70
Happy sheets, 23
Hard skills, 6, 7
Health care, 39
Helping professions, ix, xiii, 51, 142, 149, 150, 160, 167

Hierarchically organised goals, 41
Honey and Mumford learning
  styles, 53

I
Ideal futures, 42
Identity exploration, 24
Illustrative cases, xv
Imagery, 99
Impact, ix, xv, 4–6, 10, 14–16, 22,
  27–29, 35, 36, 39, 41–43, 49,
  70, 77–79, 92–95, 133, 140,
  142, 148–150, 155–162,
  166–169, 172, 173, 180
Implementation intentions, 39
Impression management, viii, 6, 7,
  10, 86, 179
Improved safety and patient
  care, 168–171
Improving a junior doctor support
  service, 170
Improving a medical equipment safety
  protocol, 170–171
Improving performance
  management, 171–173
Improving sales figures, 174–175
Inaccurate self-perceptions, 72
Increasing asbestos safety, 169–170
Indicators of progress, 107
Inductive approach, 39
Influencing others, 11
Ingham, H., 70, 71
Intelligence, 66, 78, 167
Intensity, 105
Intention, 101
Internal self-awareness, 70
Internship, 7, 15, 75, 86, 94, 143,
  154, 179
Interpersonal skills, ix, 6–11, 15, 16,
  23, 36, 68, 79, 80, 95, 114, 127,
  141, 155, 159, 160, 171,
  173, 178

Intrapersonal skills, 7
Introspection, 67, 69
Introvert, 76, 86
Introverted, 126

J
Job applications, xv, 86, 144
The Johari Window, 70
Journaling, 15, 56, 58

K
Kirkpatrick model, 27
Knowles, M., 25
Kolb's cycle, 53
Kuhn, Manford H., 72

L
Latham, Gary, x, 38, 39, 41,
  89, 114
Lazarus, Richard, 140
Leader development, 34, 168
Leader potential, 52
Leadership, ix, xiii, xix, 6, 7, 9, 10, 15,
  23, 27, 39, 52, 66, 77, 86, 102,
  125, 162, 166–168, 171, 172,
  174, 178
Leadership skills, 6, 15, 66, 86, 125,
  166, 168
Learning, viii, ix, xv, 6, 21–29, 37, 50,
  51, 53, 55, 60, 74, 79, 88, 133,
  140, 147, 154, 158, 160, 161,
  163, 171, 178–180
Learning transfer, 128
Level of conscious awareness, 41
Life pressures, 144
Life skills, 6
Listening, 50, 99, 102, 108, 126, 132,
  159, 169, 170
Lived experience, 50
Locke, Edwin, 38, 39, 41, 89, 114

Logs, 55
Long-term goals, 120
Looking-glass self, 68
Luft, J., 70, 71

M
Machiavellian, 9, 10
Making and refusing requests, 115
Maladaptive responses, 36
Marschalka, Eszter, 42
Mastery goals, 155
MBA, 13
McPartland, Thomas S., 72
Measurement of goals, 5, 8, 14, 15, 29, 106, 107, 116–117, 119, 122, 132, 145–147, 150
Mediators, 6, 38, 39, 42
Meditation, 58, 129, 131, 160
Mentoring, 25
Mezirow, Jack, 26
Mid-term goals, 120
Midwifery, 51
Mindfulness, 37, 58, 146, 160
Mindfulness techniques, 37, 160
Mindful transfer, 24
Mindset, 7, 59, 106, 129, 131, 147, 157
Mirroring, 11, 12
Mood boards, 105
Moral duty, 167
Morisano, D., 15, 42, 154
Myers Briggs Type Indicator, 71

N
Narrative, 57, 76, 154
Negative affect, 69
New Year's resolutions, 128
Non-specific outcomes, 160
Non-verbal communication, 95
Non-work lives, 35
Nursing, 51

O
Objective evidence, 156
OCD, 145
The Office, 66
Ongoing monitoring of goals, 44, 141
Ongoing written reflection, 6, 14, 41, 42, 44, 49, 51, 118, 148, 177, 178, 180
Online narrative goal-setting intervention, 42
Open-mindedness, 54
Optimism, 37, 157
Organisational goals, 89

P
Passive behaviour, 89
Pedagogy, 29
People pleaser, 104
Pennebaker, James, 15, 42, 57, 148, 154
Perceived behavioural control, 101
Perceived control, 144
Perceptual bias, 55
Performance appraisal, 11, 172
Performance gap, 5, 108, 145
Perseverance, 142, 162
Personal development, vii–ix, xv, xix, 3, 4, 10, 13, 16, 21, 29, 39, 41, 49, 51–53, 55, 60, 65, 73, 159, 168–175, 177–180
Personal disclosure, 71
Personal growth, 39, 40, 172
Personality factors, 142
Personality tests, 4, 13, 143
Personal mastery, 129
Personal resources, 140, 150
Physiological symptoms of anxiety, 100
Plato, 49
Pomodoro' technique, 158
Positive psychology interventions, 154
Positive self-talk, 100

Positive thinking, 147
Post experience, 6, 7
Postgraduate, xiii, 6, 23
Practice grounds, 5, 127, 129, 147
Pre-intervention, 42
Previous successes and failures, 101–102
Prioritisation, 103
Process goals, 37
Process measure, 28
Process- or performance-orientated, 41
Procrastination, 153, 154, 158
Progress measures, 28
Project management, 12
Proximal issues, 155
Proximity in time, 40
Psychological distress, 141
Psychometrics, 4
Psycho-Neuromuscular Theory, 99
Public speaking, 98, 100, 134, 135
Putting goals into practice, 5, 128–129

Q
Quantitative methodologies, 39
Questioning, 102

R
Rapport, 11, 129, 130
Rathus Assertiveness Scale, 114
Re-adjust goals, 131–132
Recall accuracy, 56
Reflection, xv, 9, 10, 12, 15, 24, 27, 29, 38, 47–60, 68, 69, 76, 77, 80, 87, 93, 95, 127, 135, 149, 150, 174, 180
Reflection-for-action, 51
Reflection-in-action, 9, 50, 55
Reflection-on-action, 9, 50

Reflective Goal Setting diary, 4
Reflective practice, 52
Reflective processes, 24
Reflective writing, 113, 131, 143, 148, 162
Reflexive transfer, 24
Reflexivity, 53
Repetition compulsion, 101
Resilience, ix, 34, 103, 141, 159, 173
Resilient leader, 173
Responding to criticism, 50
Retention rates, 42
Retrospection, 56
Retrospective bias, 130
'Return on Investment' (ROI), 27
Risky behaviours, 118
Role ambiguity, 144
Role model, 5, 14, 69, 103–104, 106, 114, 145
Role overload, 144
Role-play, 23

S
Satisfaction measures, 28
Schippers, M. C., 15, 42, 154
Schön, D. A., 9, 49–51
School days, 76, 86, 144
School reports, 4, 74–76
Selecting suitable goals, 4
Self-assessment tools, 143
Self-authorship, 79
Self-aware, 10, 24
Self-awareness, viii, x, 6, 9, 36, 37, 49, 52, 55, 66–75, 78, 79, 81, 119, 121, 127, 129, 141, 144, 150, 155, 161, 167, 168, 177, 179
Self-concept, 69, 76, 78, 80, 167
Self-concordant, 39, 131
Self-critical, 73, 86

Self-Determination Theory, 41
Self-discipline, 56, 127, 128, 154, 158, 160
Self-efficacy, 43, 69, 100, 129, 141, 143, 162, 166, 167, 175, 178
Self-esteem, 69, 70, 72, 88, 131, 132, 142, 143, 159
Self-generated, 41
Self-help books, 102, 145
Self-motivation, 7
Self-organisation, 157
Self-regulation, 7, 39, 44, 127, 154
Self-regulators, 13
Self-regulatory, 41
Self-report, 69, 72, 113, 114
Self-set goals, 89
Seligman's ABCDE framework (1990), 121
Semester, 141, 156, 157
Sense-making, 52, 57, 113, 150
Short-term goals, 119, 120
Significant others, 5, 41, 80–81, 94–95, 101, 106, 115, 143, 145
Sleep schedule, 112
SMART goals, 38
Social comparison theory, 70, 76
Social media, 70, 78, 80, 107, 120, 159
Social Mirror Theory, 68
Soft skills, ix, x, 4, 6, 7, 15, 16, 23, 25, 26, 29, 40, 60, 116, 167, 177, 178, 180
Soft skills development, 15, 23, 40, 178
Software developers, 180
Somatic tension, 144
Specific goal, 12, 59, 127, 146
'*Stickiness' of training*, 28
Stress, ix, xv, xix, 7, 15, 22, 34, 48–50, 70, 103, 107, 112, 113, 116, 130, 131, 139–150, 159–161, 178, 179

Stress-related theories, 140
Strong psychological theory, viii, 11, 102
Study demands, 141, 144
Study ethic, 157
Success, xv, 4–7, 15, 16, 35, 40, 41, 43, 51, 67, 70, 76, 80, 98, 101, 125, 130, 143, 146–148, 150, 157, 161, 162, 167, 178, 179
Symbolic Interactionism, 72

T
Tacit knowledge, 7
Teaching, vii, viii, 11, 26, 51, 52
Team, vii, xix, 7, 12–14, 22, 25, 50, 59, 81, 89, 90, 92–94, 108, 126, 170, 173–175, 180
Team meetings, 90
Technical skills, 6, 23, 26
Third-person perspective, 105
Thomas Kilman Conflict Style Inventory, 114
360-degree feedback, 74
Time-bounded, 38
Time-lagged quasi-experimental design, 42
Time management, 81, 130, 144, 155, 157, 158
'Tit for tat' spirals, 116
To do lists, 43
Training budgets, 23
Transferable framework, 161
Transferable skills, 7
Transfer of learning, vii, ix, xv, xix, 12, 21–29, 71, 126, 173, 179, 180
Transformational Leadership, 135
Transformational speeches, 135
Transformative Learning Theory, 26
Transitional stages, 179
Transitions, 24, 133

Traumatic experiences, 148
Twenty Statements Test, 72, 86, 88, 94

U
Unconscious priming, 36
Underachievement, 141
Undergraduate, xiii, 6, 7, 15, 23, 42, 50
Unhealthy behaviours, 142
Usage measures, 28

V
Values, 4, 9, 10, 39, 40, 53, 70, 79–80, 88, 93, 117, 120, 144, 167, 179
Video diaries, 49
Vision, 52
Visualisation, 49, 69, 98, 107, 140, 145–146
Visualise, 5, 58, 100, 112, 145

Visualising, 5, 145, 180
Visualising successful goal behaviours, 5
Vocalics, 95

W
Weight loss goal, 80
Wellbeing, 34, 35, 132, 167
Whitmore's 'Grow' Model, 180
Wholeheartedness, 54
Word processed diaries, 57
Work-life balance, 103, 113
Writing goals down, 15, 35
Written reflection, 14, 15, 42, 50, 51, 141, 162

Y
Yoga, 131, 146, 147

Z
Zimmerman, B. J., 40

Ingram Content Group UK Ltd.
Milton Keynes UK
UKHW011946140623
423431UK00001B/27